Genealogical Abstracts

from the

NEW HAMPSHIRE MERCURY

1784–1788

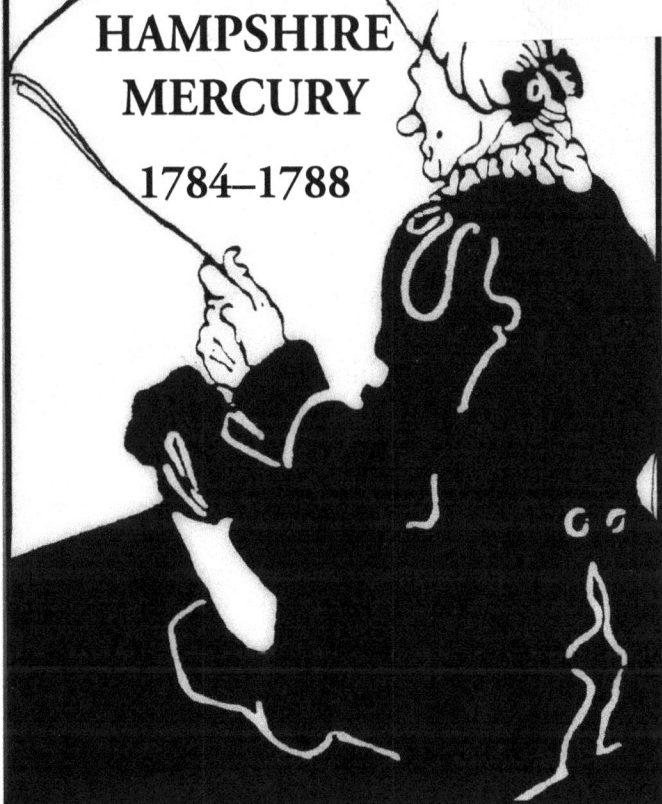

Robert Scobie

HERITAGE BOOKS
2019

HERITAGE BOOKS
AN IMPRINT OF HERITAGE BOOKS, INC.

Books, CDs, and more—Worldwide

For our listing of thousands of titles see our website
at
www.HeritageBooks.com

Published 2019 by
HERITAGE BOOKS, INC.
Publishing Division
5810 Ruatan Street
Berwyn Heights, Md. 20740

Heritage Books by the author:
Genealogical Abstracts from the New Hampshire Mercury, *1784–1788*
Genealogical Abstracts from the New Hampshere Spy, *1786–1793*
CD: *Genealogical Abstracts from the* New Hampshire Spy, *1786–1793*

International Standard Book Numbers
Paperbound: 978-0-7884-0717-8
Clothbound: 978-0-7884-6935-0

Contents

Introduction

This book is a collection of abstracts of genealogical interest which appeared in the *New Hampshire Mercury*. This newspaper was published weekly by Robert Gerrish from December 24, 1784, to March 12, 1788. His printing office was located on Congress Street in Portsmouth, New Hampshire. The issues of the *New Hampshire Mercury* were placed on microfilm by READEX, 58 Pine Street, New Canaan, CT, 06840-5408, as part of their Early American Newspaper series. With the exception of the issues listed below, the collection was complete and very readable.

Missing:
> Vol. I, No. 8, February 8, 1785
> Vol. I, No. 9, February 15, 1785
> Vol. I, No. 10, February 22, 1785
> Vol. I, No. 18, April 19, 1785
> Vol. II, No. 96, October 11, 1786
> Issue for September 6, 1787
> Vol. III, No. 160, January 16, 1788
> Vol. III, No. 164, February 13, 1788

Partially Missing:
> Vol. I, No 11, March 1, 1785

Omitted in numbering:
> Vol. II, No. 83
> Vol. III, No. 143
> Vol. III, No. 144

Listed twice:
> Vol. III, No. 122, April 11, 1787
> Vol. III, No. 122, April 18, 1787
> Vol. III, No. 141, August 30, 1787
> Vol. III, No. 141, September 13, 1787

Misnumbered:

> Vol. III, No. 145, September 27, 1787 should be Vol. III, No. 149

Mr. Gerrish charged his readers two shillings and three pence per quarter for the *New Hampshire Mercury*. He set out to provide a newspaper that was not crowded with advertisements. However, the mix between news and advertising was about the same as other New Hampshire papers of that time. Also as was the custom, foreign news items were printed first followed by national and then local news items. Most of the local news related to Portsmouth. However, significant events in the remainder of New Hampshire, northern Massachusetts and southern Maine (which was part of Massachusetts at the time) were also reported.

There are few reports of vital records. The majority of those reported were deaths with next of kin noted in most cases. Also there are many articles relating to the settlement of estates of the recently departed. Some marriages were reported along with the location and minister. Births were not reported.

Most of the other articles do not contain such direct genealogical information. However, these articles contain a wide variety of information which may provide useful clues to a genealogist. These articles include such items as:

* Advertisements
* Lists of office holders
* Collectors of excise
* Reports of crimes
* Requests for town meetings
* Reports of runaways
* Results of elections
* Dissolutions of companies
* Announcements of new businesses
* Letters held at the post office
* Houses for sale and rent
* Announcements of public auction
* Fraternal organizations, meetings and members
* Announcements of rewards

* Court actions
* Militia musters and orders
* Results of court martials
* Lists of military, civil and ecclesiastical departments
* Post rider schedules
* Alarm lists

As Portsmouth was a significant port in the late 1700s, there are many articles relating to shipping. These have the heading "Ship News." Some relate how vessels were shipwrecked. Others tell of ships being readied for sea. However, most of the articles relate to ships arriving or departing the harbor. In these abstracts, the first column is the vessel name, the second is the master's name and the third is the port from which the vessel came (ENTERED FROM) or the port of next call (CLEARED FOR).

Please note that numbers in the index correspond to the abstract number and not to a page number. Each abstract ends with a citation indicating in which newspaper issue the article appeared. This citation can be decoded as follows: volume, number, and month/day/year.

Information in the abstracts provides the reader not only valuable genealogical information but also a general understanding of life in Portsmouth, New Hampshire, in the late 1700s. I hope that you find this volume both interesting and informative.

Robert Scobie
Merritt Island, Florida

New Hampshire Mercury

December 24, 1784, to March 12, 1788

1.   The publisher, Robert Gerrish, notes that the *New Hampshire Mercury* will be sent to customers in the same manner and price that he lately did with the *New Hampshire Gazette*. The paper will be published each Friday. The *Mercury* will not be crowded with advertisements so as to leave room for important news and information. (1,1 12/24/1784)

2.   Capt. Revel, in a brig homeported in Salem, ran aground on Plum Island in a storm last Saturday, on his way to the West Indies. (1,1 12/24/1784)

3.   At his printing office on Congress Street, next to the Buck and Glove, R. Gerrish has Sewell's almanac for the year 1785 for sale. (1,1 12/24/1784)

4.   Gilbert Horney will sail for Europe this month. All persons with accounts open with him are asked to settle same. He also has rigging and other goods for sale. Portsmouth, December 1784. (1,1 12/24/1784)

5.   On December 9, it was reported that Abiel Foster of New Hampshire and Samuel Holten and George Partridge of Massachusetts were among the delegates at the United States Congress convened in Trenton, New Jersey. (1,1 12/24/1784)

6.   Francis Blood, on behalf of the committee, announces that the excise on spirituous liquors in Hillborough County from October 1784 to October 1785 will be sold at public auction at the home of Jonathan Smith, innkeeper in Amherst, on the second Tuesday of January. Amherst, December 15, 1784. (1,1 12/24/1784)

7.   White oak timbers for ship building are wanted by Mr. Peck for the shipyard in Kittery. He will pay cash for lumber delivered to the landing in Portsmouth. His office is next to R. Gerrish's printing office on Congress Street.   Portsmouth, December 21, 1784. (1,1 12/24/1784)

8.   Joshua Brackett, Joseph Bass and Jeremiah Libbey have been appointed as Commissioners to the estate of Thomas Penhallow, late of Portsmouth, merchant, deceased, represented insolvent. They will carry out this business at the post office in Portsmouth on the last Monday of the next six months. Portsmouth, December 20, 1784. (1,1 12/24/1784)

9.   Robert Gerrish has water fowl feathers for sale. Portsmouth. (1,1 12/24/1784)

10.   Thomas Manning is selling sea coal, porter, English cheese, cordage and other merchandise at his home near Liberty Bridge, Portsmouth. (1,1 12/24/1784)

11.   John Sullivan, attorney to the surviving executor, requests that all persons who have demands on the estate of Mark Wallingford, late of Somersworth, gentleman, deceased, attend a meeting at the home of Capt. Thomas Wallingford, in Somersworth, on January 5, 1785, in order to settle accounts. (1,1 12/24/1784)

12.   David Folsom has an assortment of winter and other goods for sale at his shop near the market.   Portsmouth, December 23, 1784. (1,1 12/24/1784)

13. Died: At Litchfield, NH, Wiseman Claggett, Barrister at Law, and formerly King's Attorney. (1,1 12/24/1784)

14. Ship News:

		ENTERED FROM
Brig *Kitty*	Thwing	Hispaniola
		CLEARED FOR
Schooner *Industry*	Amazeen	West Indies
Brig *Betsy*	Wishart	West Indies
Brig *Lovely Lady*	Whitehouse	Barbados
Brig *Lydia*	Brown	Demerara
Ship *Joshua*	Clarke	Antigua

(1,1 12/24/1784)

15. William Slade has an assortment of goods for sale at his recently opened shop, which is located opposite Samuel Bowles's on State Street. (1,1 12/24/1784)

16. Margaret Brewster, having suffered much damage and theft of her fence, will as of this date prosecute any person crossing her land. Portsmouth, December 29, 1784. (1,2 12/31/1784)

17. John Shute, Executor, requests that all persons with demands against the estate of Michael Shute, late of Newmarket, deceased, present their demands for prompt settlement. Newmarket, December 17, 1784. (1,2 12/31/1784)

18. Died: Lovelace Love recently in Brookhill, Ireland. He weighed 560 pounds. At Portsmouth, a child of Capt. Mumford and two children of Jeremiah Knoocks. (1,2 12/31/1784)

19. Ship News:

		ENTERED FROM
Schooner *Blossom*	Trefethen	Philadelphia
Brig *Two Brothers*	Haggens	Martinico
		CLEARED FOR
Sloop *Fair Play*	York	West Indies
Ship *George*	Tibbets	West Indies
Brig *America*	Ricker	West Indies

(1,2 12/31/1784)

20.   Nathan Nichols has the best quality New England rum for sale at his distillary in Portsmouth. (1.2 12/31/1784)

21.   William Weeks, James Brackett and Thomas Berry, acting as the committee to hire soldiers for the town of Greenland, sent a note to James Kennistone, via John Folsom, of Stratham, stating that he must serve for three years in the army of Greenland. He has not complied, so the committee cautions all persons from buying the note as it is not due and will not be paid. Greenland, December 30, 1784. (1,2 12/31/1784)

22.   Nath. Adams, Clerk, announced on November 24, 1784, that the Superior Court in Hillsborough County will be adjourned from the last Tuesday in February to the first Tuesday in May. (1,3 1/7/1785)

23.   Nathaniel Peabody, for the committee, announces that the excise for spirituous liquors for Rockingham County from October 1784 to October 1785 will be sold at an auction to be held at the home of James Thurston, innholder in Exeter, on January 18. Exeter, December 20, 1784. (1,3 1/7/1785)

24.   Cornelius Bradford and Elijah Cook, Commissioners appointed, by Jonathan Bowman, Judge of Probate, to receive claims against the estate of Jacob Davis, late of Meduncook, Lincoln County, Massachusetts, yeoman, deceased, represented insolvent, will hear claims at the home of Capt. Cornelius Bradford in Meduncook on the second Tuesday of the next six months. Meduncook Plantation, January 3, 1785. (1,3 1/7/1785)

25.   Last Friday a schooner from Salem, Capt. Diver, struck a ledge a mile off shore of Cape Elizabeth. It has since drifted into Broad Sound where it was stove to pieces. The captain and crew were saved by boat. (1,3 1/7/1785)

26. Ship News:

		CLEARED FOR
Ship *Alexander*	Ewers	Cape Francois
Brig *Honest Friend*	Moore	Madeira
Schooner *Betsey*	Andrews	Martinico

(1,3 1/7/1785)

27. Ship News:

		ENTERED FROM
Brig *Peggy*	Conn	Halifax
Schooner *Friendship*	Chamberlain	Jamaica
Schooner *Dolphin*	Clark	Connecticut
		CLEARED FOR
Brig *Mary*	Shores	Tobago
Ship *Generous Friend*	Hall	Antigua
Brig *Dragon*	Gardner	Antigua
Brig *Lucy*	Choate	Hispaniola
Sloop *Betsy*	Trundy	N. Carolina

(1,4 1/14/1785)

28. Died: At Portsmouth, Mrs. Abigail Cotton, 59, wife of Thomas Cotton; and a small child of James Melcher. (1,4 1/14/1785)

29. Aaron Hill continues to sell British goods at this wholesale and retail store on Paved Street, Portsmouth. (1,4 1/14/1785)

30. John Weeks will move from his home on January 17 and desires all persons to settle debts with him before then. Greenland, January 8, 1785. (1,4 1/14/1785)

31. Edmund H. Quincy has imported stationery for sale at his store opposite the post office. (1,4 1/14/1785)

32. Samuel Storer has a variety of English and West India goods for sale at his store on Spring Hill, next door to the market. (1,5 1/21/1785)

33. On January 17, 1785, John Moulton, Properties Clerk, town of Moultonborough, at the request of Jonathan Moulton,

Josiah Moulton and Edward B. Moulton, called a meeting of the proprietors of Moultonborough to be held at the home of Widow Leavitt, innholder in Hampton, on January 31. The meeting is to set tax rate, form a committee to fix the boundary between Sandwich and Moultonborough and conduct other business. (1,5 1/21/1785)

34.   The *New Hampshire Mercury* will now be published on Tuesdays. (1,5 1/21/1785)

35.   Ship News: CLEARED FOR
Schooner *Mary*   Welsh   St. Johns
Brig *Jane and Elizabeth* Frazer   Grenada
Schooner *Wentworth*   Marshall   Antigua
(1,5 1/21/1785)

36.   Richard Wibird Penhallow has Narragansett cheeses for sale at his store on Long Wharf. (1,5 1/21/1785)

37.   On January 17, 1785, Josiah Moulton, Proprietors Clerk for the town of Tamworth, at the request of Jonathan Moulton, John Moulton and Edward B. Moulton, called a meeting of the proprietors of Tamworth to be held at the home of Widow Leavitt, innholder of Hampton, on January 31. The meeting is to form a committee to set the boundary between Tamworth and Sandwich, set a tax rate and conduct other business. (1,5 1/21/1785)

38.   James Underwood and Samuel Chase have been appointed Commissioners to the estate of Joseph Barnes, late of Litchfield, physician, deceased, represented insolvent. They will conduct business at the home of Joseph Barnes in Litchfield on the second Tuesday of the next six months. Litchfield, January 11, 1785. (1,5 1/21/1785)

39.   Benjamin Parker and William Moore, Commissioners, appointed by Joseph Simpson, Judge of Probate of Wills etc. in York County, to examine claims against the estate of Capt. Robert Follett, late of Kittery, mariner, deceased, represented

insolvent will hear the claims at the home of Mary Follett, in Kittery on the first Wednesday of the next five months. Kittery, January 23, 1785. (1,6 1/25/1785)

40. Ship News:

		CLEARED FOR
Brig *Rambler*	Ober	Carolina
Brig *Hephzibah*	Adams	West Indies
Ship *Pilgram*	Tuck	West Indies

(1,6 1/25/1785)

41. Died: At Portsmouth, Mrs. Sarah Daverson, 41, wife of Thomas Daverson, of Portsmouth, and their infant child. (1,6 1/25/1785)

42. Died: At Portsmouth, a two year old child of Capt. David Cullum. (1,7 2/1/1785)

43. Ship News:

		ENTERED FROM
Schooner *Flying Fish*	Clark	St. Johns
		CLEARED FOR
Sloop *Adonis*	Long	St. Vincents
Sloop *Statira*	Manning	Barbados

(1,7 2/1/1785)

44. By license from Phillips White, Judge of Probate, etc., of Rockingham County, Noah Emery Jr., Administrator to the estate, will hold a public auction at the home of Benjamin Lamson, innholder in Exeter, on February 24, a farm. This farm is part of the estate of Dr. Nathaniel Gilman, late of Exeter, deceased. This farm lies within a mile of the meeting house in Exeter. It contains about 100 acres and has a house, barn and one-quarter of a saw mill in Brentwood. February 1, 1785. (1,7 2/1/1785)

45. The General Court of New Hampshire chose Rev. Jeremy Belknap, of Dover, to preach the next election sermon. (1,11 3/1/1785)

46.   Died: At Portsmouth, Mrs. Abigail Ham, 85; a child of George Walden; and Mrs. Jean Gentleman, 50. (1,11 3/1/1785)

47.   A boy, about 15, claiming to be Otis Varney of Rochester came to a home in Portsmouth about ten days ago to seek employment. (1,11 3/1/1785)

48.   Several of Major General Sullivan's addresses on the militia are for sale at R. Gerrish's printing office.   (1,11 3/1/1785)

49.   John Gould will trade English and West India goods for good pine boards delivered to him in Portsmouth.   (1,11 3/1/1785)

50.   A 140-acre farm in Kittery is for sale. It has 60 acres of woods and is 12 miles from the river. Contact Paul or Mark Lord of Berwick for more details. Portsmouth, February 21, 1785. (1,11 3/1/1785)

51.   G. Doig has a genteel chaise complete with harness for sale. (1,11 3/1/1785)

52.   William Brewster has a large double house for sale or rent. It also has a barn, wood house, well, and large garden. It is located on the street leading from the market to Col. Wentworth's and is occupied by Stephen Hardy.   (1,11 3/1/1785)

53.   James Hill notes that all persons having accounts with the late company of Shute and Hill in Newmarket should settle them promptly. Newmarket, February 6, 1785. (1,11 3/1/1785)

54.   Yesterday a town meeting was held in Portsmouth to vote for state President and senators. Results in descending order were as follows: for President George Atkinson, John Langdon, General Sullivan and Woodbury Langdon. For Senator Joseph Gilman, George Atkinson, Joshua Wentworth, Samual Hale, Christopher Toppan, John Langdon, Thomas Odiorne, John

McClary, Woodbury Langdon and John Bell. (1,12 3/8/1785)

55. Died: At Stratham, on March 3, Rev. Mr. Adams of Stratham after a tedious illness at an advanced age. (1,12 3/8/1785)

56. Ship News: CLEARED FOR
Brig *Carbonear*   Briard   West Indies
(1,12 3/8/1785)

57. At town meetings in Keene and other towns near the Connecticut River, John Langdon has received almost unanimous votes for President of New Hampshire. (1,13 3/15/1785)

58. Ship News: ENTERED FROM
Brig *Hermoine*   Mountford   Port-au-Prince
                                            CLEARED FOR
Schooner *Industry*   Landsfield   Shelburne
Brig *Peggy*   Conn   Mountserrat
(1,13 3/15/1785)

59. Died: At Portsmouth, Mrs. Mary McCarty, 74. (1,13 3/15/1785)

60. Aaron Hill has English goods for sale at his store on Moffatt's wharf. (1,13 3/15/1785)

61. Died: At Portsmouth, Abraham Bartlet, 93. (1,14 3/22/1785)

62. Ship News: ENTERED FROM
Schooner *Swallow*   Smith   Baltimore
Ship *Chalkley*   Fernald   Barbados
(1,14 3/22/1785)

63. Thomas Martin, John Parker and Daniel R. Rogers, having been appointed Commissioners, by Phillips White, will examine the claims against the estate of Alexander Henderson, late of

Portsmouth, merchant, deceased, represented insolvent. They will conduct business on the last Wednesday of the next six months at the home of Capt. William Brewster. Portsmouth, March 21, 1785. (1,14 3/22/1785)

64.   Daniel Beebe, a Justice of the Peace for Strafford County, has granted the request of Moses Weed, Elisha Weed, Nathaniel Weed, Orlando Weed, and Orlando Weed Jr. for Moses Senter, proprietors of Burton, to hold a town meeting on the fourth Wednesday of May at the home of Elisha Weed in Burton. At the meeting, town officials will be elected and a tax rate established. (1,14 3/22/1785)

65.   Samuel Mooers and Walter Robie, Commissioners, appointed by Phillips White, Judge of Probate for Rockingham County, will examine claims against the estate of Coffin Mooers, late of Candia, physician, deceased, represented insolvent. They will conduct business on the last Thursday of the next six months at the home of Samuel Mooers, innholder, in Candia. Candia, March 17, 1785. (1,14 3/22/1785)

66.   Mesech Weare, President of New Hampshire, notes that Charles Hellstedt has been recognized as Consul in the United States for the King of Sweden. As such he is granted the rights and the privileges that accompany the position. The notice was signed by E. Thompson, Secretary. (1,15 3/29/1785)

67.   Ship News:

		ENTERED FROM
Brig *Adventure*	Odiorne	Antigua
		CLEARED FOR
Brig *Cooner*	White	West Indies

(1,15 3/29/1785)

68.   E. H. Quincy has Lisbon lemons for sale at his store opposite the post office. Portsmouth, March 29. (1,15 3/29/1785)

69.   Francis Drew of Newmarket, Newfields is offering lessons for drummers and fifers. Newmarket, March 24, 1785. (1,15 3/29/1785)

70. The public is warned against purchasing continental securities signed by John Pierce, Commissioner, as many have been counterfeited. (1,16 4/5/1785)

71. Died: At Portsmouth, Capt. John Yeaton, 38; Mrs. Hannah Lear, 36, wife of Samuel Lear, of Portsmouth; and a child of John Libbey. (1,16 4/5/1785)

72. Ship News:

		ENTERED FROM
Brig *Ganganelli*	Stacy	Hispaniola
		CLEARED FOR
Brig *Kitty*	Twing	West Indies
Brig *Two Brothers*	Haggens	West Indies
Brig *George & Jane*	Vennard	West Indies

(1,16 4/5/1785)

73. Peter Pearse has a few bags of sea fowl feathers for sale. (1,16 4/5/1785)

74. Benja. Dearborn, auctioneer, will auction a twenty-five ton schooner next Wednesday at Warner's Wharf. Portsmouth, April 1, 1785. (1,16 4/5/1785)

75. Benjamin Dearborn will start a vocal singing school for young ladies starting on April 19. Portsmouth, April 5, 1785. (1,16 4/5/1785)

76. The following men were elected to the offices noted at a town meeting in Portsmouth on March 25, 1785:
Town Clerk — John Evans
Selectmen — Nathaniel Folsom, John Sparhawk, John Noble, Capt. William Gardner, Capt. Peter Cowes
Overseers of the Poor — General Whipple, Dr. John Jackson, Samuel Bowles, Jeremiah Libby, Ichabod Nichols
Assessors — Samuel Penhallow, Ammi R. Cutter, Samuel Sherburne, John Furnald, Thomas Sheafe
Auditors — John Sherburne, John Parker, Joshua Wentworth
Firewards — John Sherburne, Daniel Rindge, John Parker, Woodbury Langdon, John Langdon, Capt. George

Wentworth, Joshua Wentworth, Nathaniel Folsom, Jacob Treadwell, Ichabod Nichols, Jacob Sheafe Jr., Jeremiah Libbey

Attorneys — John Pickering, Oliver Whipple

Agents — Samuel Cutts, Samuel Penhallow

Keeper of the Magazine — Jeremiah Libbey

To enquire who kills deer out of season — Capt. George Wentworth

Fence Viewers — Samuel Sherburne, Joseph Tucker, Samuel Hall, Abraham Elliot, William Ham, Walter Akerman

Lot Layers — Samuel Hale, William Hart, Nathaniel Adams,

Constables — Clement March, George Ham Jr., Thomas Chadbourn, Stacy Hall

Searchers and Sealers of Leather — George Dame, Nathaniel Jackson, Perkins Ayers

Cullers of Staves and Packers of Fish — Joseph Walton, George Howe, George Hull, John Pitman

Pound Keeper — Thomas Bryent

Surveyors of Boards and Measurers of Timber — Samuel Hutchings, William Wilson, John Beck, Moses Noble

Hog Reaves — William Walden, Charles Waters, Samuel Ham (Plains), Levi Wiggins, Joseph Wincoll

Measurers of Wood by Land and Water — John Beck, William Yeaton, Schackford Seaward, Samuel Beck, Ephraim Dennett, Henry Sherburne, John Melcher, William Moses

Corders of Wood — Joseph Benson, William Walden, Thomas Priest, Richard Peverly, Samuel Jones, George Walden

Sealer of Weights and Measures — Daniel Lunt

(1,17 4/12/1785)

77. Ship News:

		ENTERED FROM
Schooner *Industry*	Amazeen	St. Eustatia
Brig *Susannah*	Parker	Tobago
Ship *Atlantic*	Trefethen	Grenada
		CLEARED FOR
Ship *Chalkley*	Stokell	West Indies
Ship *Elizabeth*	Seaward	Bristol
Brig *Hermoine*	White	West Indies

Brig *Nancy*   Peirce   West Indies
(1,17 4/12/1785)

78. William Brewster is planning to open a stable. Anyone interesting in using same should see him at Brewster's Tavern. Portsmouth, April 7, 1785. (1,17 4/12/1785)

79. William Appleton has fresh lemons for sale. (1,17 4/12/1785)

80. Ebenezer Sullivan has a schooner, suitable for fishing or offshore trade, for sale. Durham, April 6, 1785. (1,17 4/12/1785)

81. David Folsom has a general assortment of European goods for sale at his store near the market in Portsmouth. (1,19 4/26/1785)

82. Those desiring New Hampshire certificates or New Hampshire state notes that can be exchanged with Massachusetts, should contact William Brewster. (1,19 4/26/1785)

83. Ebenezer Thompson Jr., of Durham, has two 15-ton fishing schooners for sale. (1,19 4/26/1785)

84. Because the roads are impassable, John White has delayed the start of his school on minuet dancing until May 3. (1,19 4/26/1785)

85. Ship News: Yesterday a brig, Capt. Riley, arrived in 17 days from St. Kitts. (1,19 4/26/1785)

86. Married: At Exeter, William Woodbridge, Preceptor to the academy there, to Miss Betsy Brooks, daughter of Deacon Brooks, of that place. (1,19 4/26/1784)

87. Died: At Portsmouth, Mrs. Hannah Chandler, 38, wife of Benjamin Chandler, of Portsmouth. (1,19 4/26/1785)

88.   Ship News: ENTERED FROM
Schooner *Betsy Manning*   St. Kitts
Sloop *Adonis*   Long   St. Eustatia
(1,19 4/26/1785)

89. The following letters are being held at the Portsmouth post office as of April 23:

•A: Joshua Atherton, Amherst.

•B: John Bevens, Wendell; Joseph Blanchard, Chester; James Bean, Brintwood.

•C: Samuel Cutts (2), Portsmouth; Wiseman Claggett, Portsmouth; Rev. Curtis Coe, Durham; James Caies, Dover; Robert Calder, Wolfeboro; Rev. Mr. Cassett, Claremont; T. Cogswell, Gilmanton.

•D: Joseph Doe, Newmarket; A. M'Dairmin, Thornton.

•E: John Ewins, Londonderry.

•F: William Frost, III, Berwick; John Fletcher (2), Thornton.

•H: Hohn Haggens, Berwick; Nath. Hooper, Berwick; James Hamilton, Portsmouth; John Hole, Portsmouth; Samuel Huntly, Lemister.

•J: David Jones, Lemister.

•K: Hugo Kennijon, Kittery; James Lock, Burnstead.

•L: Gideon Lamson, Exeter.

•M: Joha. Moulton, Hampton; Eliza Moody, Newmarket; Duncan M. Naughton, Newmarket; Rev. S. Moore, New Boston; Rev. David McClure, North Hampton; John McLullan, Thornton; James March, Portsmouth.

•P: Peirce & Dix, Peterboro; Nath. Peabody, Atkinton; Robert Parkes, Exeter; Joseph Prime, Berwick; Robert Parker, Portsmouth.

•R: Ichabod Rollings, Portsmouth.

•S: John Sullivan, Durham; Richard Seaman, Portsmouth; Jacob Shurburn, Loudon; Gen. Stark, Londonderry.

•T: Henry Trefethen, Portsmouth; Thomas Tab, New Durham; Joseph Tilton, Exeter; Daniel Tenny, Hopkinton; John Tanner, Portsmouth; Mathew Tracey, Portsmouth.

•W: Rev. Simeon Williams, Windham.

Note: Spelling of names is as found on the letters.
(1,19 4/26/1785)

90. Joseph Bass has an assortment of garden seeds for sale at his shop in Portsmouth. (1,19 4/26/1785)

91. Ship News: Last Sunday, the ship *Thomas*, Capt. Theodore Furber, arrived from England via Lisbon. Furber spoke to the sloop *Betsy*, Samuel Edwards, off Cape Sable, all is well. (1,20 5/3/1785)

92. Died: At Portsmouth, James March, 57, joiner. He left a wife and ten children. (1,20 5/3/1785)

93. Ship News:

		ENTERED FROM
Brig *Endeavor*	Riley	St. Eustatia
Ship *Thomas*	Furber	Lisbon
		CLEARED FOR
Sloop *Polly*	Lear	Baltimore

(1,20 5/3/1785)

94. Theodore Furber has good Lisbon salt for sale on board the ship *Thomas*, which is at Capt. Woodbury Langdon's wharf. (1,20 5/3/1785)

95. Died: At Portsmouth, Capt. John Briard, 83, of Portsmouth; Mrs. Ann Shannon, 46, of Portsmouth, comfort of Nathaniel Shannon; Mrs. Elizabeth Stokell, 38, comfort of Capt. John Stokell, of Portsmouth. (1,21 5/10/1785)

96. Ship News:

		ENTERED FROM
Schooner *Endeavor*	Harden	Maryland
Brig *Abigail*	Peirce	Grenada
Brig *Dragon*	Gardner	West Indies
		CLEARED FOR
Ship *Jane*	Bickford	West Indies
Sloop *Mary*	Garrison	West Indies

(1,21 5/10/1785)

97. Goddard and Storer have a general assortment of painter's colors and supplies for sale. (1,21 5/10/1785)

98. Jonathan Moulton of Hampton has for rent, for three years, a house and necessary buildings at Center Harbor in New Hampton. This house which is suitable for a public tavern is located on 50 acres of land. Hampton 27, 1785. (1,21 5/10/1785)

99. On June 2, an auction will be held on the premises to sell 1000 acres of land at the head of navigation of the Kennebeck River. This is well suited for a farmer, trader or merchant. Profits will be used to offset the debts of the estate of Brigs Hallowell, late of Hallowell, deceased. For particulars contact Prentice Hallowell, Administratix of the estate, at Samuel Bonner's on Long Lane in Boston or Jonathan Bowman at Pownelborough. (1,22 5/17/1785)

100. Died: At Portsmouth, Samuel Waters, 82; William Appleton, 38; a child of Daniel Peirce; an infant of Jeremiah Hill and an infant of Thomas Neal. (1,22 5/17/1785)

101. Ship News:		ENTERED FROM
Sloop *Fair Play*	York	St. Lucia
		CLEARED FOR
Brig *Mary*	Odiorne	West Indies
Schooner *Betsy*	Salter	Demerara
Sloop *Adonis*	Drisco	West Indies

(1,22 5/17/1785)

102. Joshua Howard, Andrew S. Crocker and Nathaniel Merrill have been appointed Commissioners to examine claims against the estate of Thomas Simpson, late of Haverhill, NH, deceased, represented insolvent. They will conduct business at the home of Andrew S. Crocker in Haverhill on the third Tuesday of the next six months. Haverhill, May 6, 1785. (1,22 5/17/1785)

103. Joshua Brackett, Joseph Bass and Jeremiah Libbey have been appointed Commissioners to settle claims against the estate of Thomas Penhallow, late of Portsmouth, merchant, deceased, represented insolvent. They will conduct business at the post office in Portsmouth on the last Monday of this month.

Portsmouth, May 17, 1785. (1,22 5/17/1785)

104. John Costelloe have sundry tracts of land for sale in Marlboro, Fitzwilliam, Parkersfield, Stoddard, Washington, Fishersfield, New London, Hillsboro, New Bradford, Mason, Rindge, Jaffery, Dublin, Peterborough, Lyndboro, New Boston, Weare, Andover, Alexandria, New Chester, Camble's Gore, Kiersarge Gore, and Meredith Gore. These lots have been willed to Costelloe from Col. Wallingford. Effingham, May 14, 1785. (1,22 5/17/1785)

105. Died: At Conway on May 12, the wife of Eliphalet Danford, of that town, cut her own throat while in bed with her husband. She died immediately. (1,23 5/24/1785)

106. Died: At Portsmouth, Capt. James Hickey, 49. At sea, Stephen Nichols in a fall from the main yard of the brig *Neptune*, Capt. Spence. Nichols landed in the water and drowned. (1,23 5/24/1785)

107. Ship News

		ENTERED FROM
Brig *Neptune*	Spence	St. Eustatia
Schooner *Union*	Salter	St. Martin
Brig *Carbonear*	Briard	Nevis
Brig *Mary*	Shores	Tobago
		CLEARED FOR
Ship *Atlantic*	Trefethen	West Indies
Brig *Bee*	Fletcher	West Indies
Sloop *Betsey*	Smith	Baltimore
Brig *Susannah*	Parker	West Indies
Brig *Viscomte de Arrote*	Miller	Tobago

(1,23 5/24/1785)

108. Meshech Weare, President of New Hampshire, dissolved the General Court effective May 24. The proclamation was signed by E. Thompson, Secretary. (1,23 5/24/1785)

109. A hull of a 200 ton ship belonging to John Hurd of Boston will be auctioned on May 26. The sale will take place at the

home of Edward Emerson, innholder of York. Conditions of the sale can be obtained from Daniel Sewell of York. May 21, 1785. (1,23 5/24/1785)

110. Rev. Mr. Belknap will deliver a sermon to open the first session of the new General Court. (1,24 5/31/1785)

111. Died: At Portsmouth, Richard Wibird Penhallow, 35, eldest son of John Penhallow, of Portsmouth, merchant; and a child of Thomas Moses. (1,24 5/31/1785)

112. Ship News:

		ENTERED FROM
Brig *Home Friend*	Moore	Lisbon
		CLEARED FOR
Brig *Endeavor*	Riley	St. Bartholomew
Brig *Live Oak*	Adams	West Indies
Schooner *Dispatch*	Ham	Virginia

(1,24 5/31/1785)

113. Samuel Hill has an assortment of goods imported from London for sale at his store opposite the market in Portsmouth. (1,24 5/31/1785)

114. William Pearne has Madeira wine and other goods for sale at his store in the North End. (1,24 5/31/1785)

115. On July 7, John McCrilles will sell 200 acres of land next to his property. The auction will be held at his house in Deerfield. Deerfield, May 28, 1785. (1,24 5/31/1785)

116. A valuable farm in Stratham, where Capt. George Marsh lives, will be auctioned on June 20. The farm is within a half mile of the meeting house on a road between Portsmouth and Exeter. The farm features an almost new house. The auction will be held at the farm. (1,25 6/7/1785)

117. On June 6 a note of hand of one hundred pounds was found in Portsmouth. It was dated in Epping and was from Rhoda Swain to Dudley Prescott. With proof the owner may

claim it from Enoch Barker. (1,25 6/7/1785)

118. Died: At Portsmouth, Elias Tarlton, 95; a daughter of Mrs. Hannah Light, 9 years and 6 months. (1,25 6/7/1785)

119. Ship News: CLEARED FOR
Brig *Harmony*   Foster   West Indies
Brig *Neptune*   Spence   West Indies
(1,25 6/7/1785)

120. All persons with accounts outstanding with the estate of James Hickey, late of Portsmouth, deceased, should bring their accounts to Elizabeth Hickey, Executrix, for settlement. Portsmouth, June 14. (1,26 6/14/1785)

121. Abraham Burnham, Daniel Brainerd and Thomas Ramsey have been appointed Commissioners to the estate of Timothy Fuller, late of Rumney, deceased, represented insolvent. They will conduct their business at the home of Asa Fuller in Rumney on the first Tuesday of the next four months. Rumney, May 24, 1785. (1,26 6/14/1785)

122. On June 1, the General Court of New Hampshire convened in Portsmouth. John Sullivan was chosen Speaker of the House of Representatives. John Calfe was chosen Clerk. Then Rev. Mr. Belknap delivered a sermon.
THE MEMBERS OF THE SENATE ARE:
Rockingham County
    John McClary   Joseph Gilman
    John Langdon   George Atkinson
    Nathaniel Peabody
Strafford County
    John Wentworth   Otis Baker
Hillsborough County
    Matthew Thornton   Ebenezer Webster
Cheshire County
    Moses Chase   John Bellows
Grafton County
    Francis Worcester

The following were selected as officers in the Senate: John Taylor Gilman, Treasurer; Ebenezer Thompson, Secretary; Joseph Pearson, Deputy Secretary.

No candidate had a majority for President so the House passed the names of John Langdon and George Atkinson to the Senate for consideration. Langdon was voted to and accepted the position of President. The Senate than selected Joshua Wentworth to fill the Senate seat vacated by Langdon. Then the following were selected as Counselors for the state: Nathaniel Peabody, Matthew Thornton, John Sullivan, Amos Shephard, Moses Drew.

The following are the MEMBERS OF THE HOUSE OF REPRESENTATIVES:

Rockingham County

Portsmouth	George Atkinson
	George Gains
	John Pickering
Exeter	Josiah Gilman*
Londonderry	John Prentice*
	Arch'd McMurphy
Chester	Col. William White*
Newington	Ephraim Pickering
Greenland	William Weeks
Rye	Samuel Jenness
North Hampton	Col. Moses Leavitt*
Hampton	Christopher Toppan
Hampton Falls & Seabrook	Abner Sandborn*
Stratham	Mark Wiggin
Kensington	Moses Shaw S.
Hampton & E. Kingston	Nath'l Batcheldor
Kingston	Capt. John Eastman
Brentwood	Capt. Levi Morrill
Epping	William Plummer*
Newmarket Nottingham	Col. Thomas Bartlett
Deerfield	Moses Barnard*
Northwood, Epsom & Allenstown	
Chichester & Pittsfield	
Canterbury & Northfield	Charles Gidden*
Loudon	Nathan Batcheldor

(MEMBERS OF THE HOUSE OF REPRESENTATIVES)

Concord	Peter Green
Raymond & Poplin	
Hawke & Sandown	Thomas Page*
Hampstead Atkinson &	
Plaistow	Nathaniel Peabody
Newton Salem	Caleb Dustin*
Wyndham	James Betran
Pelham	Jacob Butler

Strafford County:

Dover	Col. John Waldron*
Durham	Gen. John Sullivan*
Somersworth	Maj. Jona. Wentworth
Rochester	James Knowles
Barrington	Capt. Joshua Foss
Sanbornton	Capt. William Harper*
Gilmanton	Col. Joseph Badger*
Lee	Dr. James Brackett
Madbury Meredith	
& New Hampton	
Sandwich &	
Tamworth	David Gilman*
Moultonboro, Tuftonboro,	
Wolfeboro &	
Ossipee	Reuben Libbey*
Barnstead,	
New Durham &	
New Durham Gore	Thomas Tash
Wakefield, Middleton	
& Effingham Conway,	
Eaton and Burton	

Hillsborough County:

Nottingham West	Samuel Marsh
Litchfield & Derryfield Dunstable	Capt. Benjamin French
Merrimac	James Martin
Bedford	Timothy Taylor*
Goffstown	Robert MacGregore
Hollis	Daniel Emerson

(MEMBERS OF THE HOUSE OF REPRESENTATIVES)

Amherst	Robert Means
Raby & Mason	Capt. Sam'l Douglas*
New Ipswich	Ephraim Adams
Duxbury &	
Mile-slip Wilton	Col. Philip Putnam
Lyndboro	Capt. Levi Spaulding
Temple &	
Peterboro-slip	
Peterboro &	
Society Land	Mathew Wallace
Hancock,	
Antrim &	
Deering	John Duncan
Henniker & Hillsboro	Maj. Robert Wallace
New Boston Weare	Jonathan Dow
Hopkinton	Benjamin Darling*
Dunbarton & Bow	John Brient
Salisbury	Robert Smith
Boscawen	George Jackman
Fisherfield,	
Sutton & Warner	Mathew Harvey*
New London,	
Andover & Gore	
Cheshire County:	
Charlestown	Elijah Grout
Alstead	Col. Amos Shepard
Keene	Benjamin Hall
Swanzey	Maj. Elisha Whitcomb
Richmond	Jonathan Gaskill*
Jaffrey	John Gilmore*
Winchester	Capt. Simon Willard
Westmoreland	Samuel Works*
Chesterfield Rindge	Edward Jewett*
Walpole Claremont	Capt. Benj'n Sumner
Cornish & Grantham	Nathan Young*
Newport & Craydon	Stephen Powers
Acworth, Lempster & Marlow	Elijah Frink
Wendell & Unity	Lemuel Holmes

(MEMBERS OF THE HOUSE OF REPRESENTATIVES)

Surry & Gilsom	Jacob Copeland
Stoddard & Washington	Samuel Griffin
Dublin & Packersfield	Samuel Kendell*
Marlboro & Fitzwilliam	Maj. Joseph Kimbell
Plainfield Protectworth & Hinsdale	

GRAFTON COUNTY:

Holderness, Copton, Thornton, Lincoln & Franconia	Noah Worcester*
Plymouth, Rumney &Wentworth	Capt. Ab'm Burnham*
New Chester, Alexandria & Cockermouth	Enoch Noyes
Enfield, Canaan, Cardigan, Dorchester &Grafton	Ebenezer Hoyt
Hanover	Russel Freeman
Lebanon	Elisha Payne
Lyme & Orford	Col. William Simpson
Haverhill, Piermont, Warren & Coventry	Col. Moses Dow*
Bath, Lyman, Landaff, Concord (alias Gunthwait), Littleton &Dalton	Maj. John Young
Lancester, Northumberland, Strafford, Dartmouth, Piercy, Cockburn &Colburn	Col. John Whipple

* indicates not of the House last year. (1,26 6/14/1785)

123. Died: At Portsmouth, Nathaniel Lang, 85. (1,26 6/14/1785)

124. Ship News:

		ENTERED FROM
Brig *Lydia*	Brown	Demerara
Brig *Cooper*	White	Guadaloupe
		CLEARED FOR
Brig *Ganganelli*	Stacy	West Indies
Brig *Dragon*	Oram	West Indies

(1,26 6/14/1785)

125. Samuel Storer has a variety of English and West India goods for sale at his store on Spring Hill next to the market. (1,26 6/14/1785)

126. Died: At Portsmouth, a Negro man of Col. Wentworth. (1,27 6/21/1785)

127. Ship News: ENTERED FROM
Brig *Betsy*   Wishart   Shelburne
Sloop *Gen. Green*   Godfrey   New York
Brig *Hermoine*   White   Martinico
Ship *Chalkley*   Stokell   St. Vincent
(1,27 6/21/1785)

128. Thomas Sheafe has Nova Scotia grindstones and an assortment of European and West India goods for sale at his store in the north end adjoining the town wharf. (1,27 6/21/1785)

129. Any person having demands on the estate of George Pierce, late of Portsmouth, mariner, deceased should settle promptly with Daniel Pierce, Administrator. Portsmouth, June 13, 1785. (1,27 6/21/1785)

130. Any person having outstanding accounts with the estate of James Hickey, late of Portsmouth, deceased, should bring them to Betty Hickey, Executrix, for settlement. Portsmouth, June 14. (1,27 6/21/1785)

131. Died: At Portsmouth, Benjamin Slade, 18. (1,28 6/28/1785)

132. Ship News: ENTERED FROM
Sloop *Eagle*   Fairchild   Connecticut
                                     CLEARED FOR
Schooner *Delight*   Peamont   St. John's
Brig *Abigail*   Peirce   West Indies
(1,28 6/28/1785)

133. Zillia Stoney and Joseph Emery by force and fraud obtained a 14 pound-8 shilling note from Richard Ellison while he was in his home. Ellison warns everyone not to purchase this document as he will not pay it. Canterbury, June 14, 1785. (1,28 6/28/1785)

134. Last Tuesday Silas Gould, 17, an apprentice, ran away from Nath'l Dean. Gould is short, well built, with darkish complexion and dark bushy hair. An $8 reward will be paid for his return. (1,29 7/5/1785)

135. The General Court passes during its last session several acts and resolutions including the following:
•Repeal an act passed on November 29, 1777 to prevent the transfer of real estate belonging to persons inimical to the United States, so far as the act respects the power of attorney given by Peter Levius to Woodbury Langdon.
•An act enabling Thomas Bartlett to sell land belonging to his wards. (1,29 7/5/1785)

136. Ship News:

		ENTERED From
Sloop *Nancy*	Williams	Connecticut
Brig *Mary*	Odiorne	Burin
		CLEARED FOR
Brig *Hope*	Lambert	West Indies
Ship *Lydia*	Tibbets	Cape Fear
Ship *Thomas*	Furber	West Indies
Brig *Maria*	Taylor	St. Eustatia
Brig *Hermoine*	White	West Indies
Brig *Carbonair*	Briard	West Indies

(1,29 7/5/1785)

137. John Noble, Nathaniel Folsom, Peter Cowes, John Sparhawk and William Gardner, Selectmen of Portsmouth, warn that mad dogs have already caused fatalities in other parts of the state. Thus any dog running loose in the limits of Portsmouth will be killed. Portsmouth, July 2, 1785. (1,29 7/5/1785)

138. Ship News: Yesterday Capt. Haggens arrived in a brig from St. Kitts. He reports that three American vessels were seized and condemned by the Court of Admirality of that island. Included was a vessel from Portsmouth commanded by Capt. Vennard. (1,30 7/12/1785)

139. The Society of Cincinnati of New Hampshire held its annual meeting last Monday in Exeter. Results of election of officers are as follows: President, Major General Sullivan; Vice President, Brig. Gen. Cilley; Secretary, Major Fogg; Treasurer, Lt. Col. McClary; and Vice Treasurer Capt. Cass. (1,30 7/12/1785)

140. The Society of Cincinnati of Massachusetts held its annual meeting last Monday in Boston. Results of election of officers are as follows: President, Major General Lincoln; Vice President, Major General Knox; and Secretary, Col. Brooks. (1,30 7/12/1785)

141. Died: At Portsmouth, Mrs. Mary Long, 42, comfort of Peirse Long. (1,30 7/12/1785)

142. Ship News:

		ENTERED FROM
Brig *Sampson*	Salter	Turks Island
		CLEARED FOR
Brig *Mary*	Shore	West Indies

(1,30 7/12/1785)

143. The meeting of proprietors of Piermont will be held next Friday at Capt. Brewster's in Portsmouth. Portsmouth, July 11, 1785. (1,30 7/12/1785)

144. Eliphalet Hale and William Parker Jr. have been appointed Commissioners, by Philips White, Judge of Wills &, to examine claims against the estate of Thomas Lord, late of Exeter, glazier, deceased, represented insolvent. They will conduct business on the first Monday of the next five months at the home of James Thurston, innholder, in Exeter. July, 8 1785. (1,30 7/12/1785)

145. Samuel Storer is offering a $30 reward for the recovery of the merchandise stolen from his store during the night of July 6. (1,30 7/12/1785)

146. Ship News:

		ENTERED FROM
Brig *Two Brothers*	Haggens	St. Eustatia
Brig *Nancy*	Peirce	Turks Island
		CLEARED FOR
Brig *Betsy*	Wishart	West Indies

(1,31 7/19/1785)

147. On July 15, a mare was stolen from William Simpson of Stratham. Anyone apprehending the thief and providing information on the mare will be rewarded by the owner. Stratham, July 16, 1785. (1,31 7/19/1785)

148. Samuel Gilman, executor, requests that anyone having claims against the estate of John Sanborn, late of Newmarket, deceased, present them to Gilman. Newmarket, July 20, 1785. (1,32 7/26/1785)

149. A lot of land in Wakefield, owned by Jonathan Allen, will be sold at public vendue on August 11 at the home of Mr. Merrill, innholder, in Greenland. Greenland, July 25, 1785. (1,32 7/26/1785)

150. Died: At Portsmouth, Mrs. Mary Libbey, 35, comfort of John Libbey, of Portsmouth; a child of Mr. Edwards. (1,32 7/26/1785)

151. Ship News:

		ENTERED FROM
Brig *Endeavor*	Riley	St. Martins
Sloop *Adonis*	Drisco	Martinico
		CLEARED FOR
Ship *Chalkley*	Furnald	West Indies

(1,32 7/26/1785)

152. A farm in Canterbury, will be sold at the home of Capt. Jeremiah Clough, innholder in Canterbury, on August 16, 1785.

The farm is one mile north of the meeting house and contains 90 acres, a dwelling house and barn. For more information contact Nicholas Mariner, who is a tenant on the farm. (1,33 8/2/1785)

153. Died: At Portsmouth, Mrs. Lydia Moses, 35, comfort of Thomas Moses, of Portsmouth; and a son, 5, of Capt. Joseph Seaward, by drowning. (1,33 8/2/1785)

154. Ship News:

		CLEARED FOR
Brig *Mary*	Odiorne	St. Peters
Brig *Honest Friend*	Moore	Western Islands
Brig *Cooper*	White	Cape Francois
Schooner *Gilman*	Bowditch	West Indies
Brig *Betsey*	Haggens	West Indies

(1,33 8/2/1785)

155. Yesterday the home of Samuel Jenness in Rye was consumed by fire which started when a spark landed on the roof. Most of the valuables were saved. (1,34 8/9/1785)

156. Died: At Portsmouth, a child of William Martin; a child of John Howe; and a child of Capt. Daniel Lang. (1,34 8/9/1785)

157. Ship News:

		ENTERED FROM
Schooner *Dispatch*	Ham	Virginia
Schooner *Betsy*	Salter	St. Eustatia
		CLEARED FOR
Brig *Hephzibeh*	Adams	Cadiz

(1,34 8/9/1785)

158. A Negro girl, named Violet, ran away from Capt. John Donaldson on August 6. A $4 reward will be given to the person returning her to Alexander Ewen. Portsmouth, August 9, 1785. (1,34 8/9/1785)

159. Died: At Portsmouth, Henry Seaward, 48. (1,35 8/16/1785)

160. On July 22, Capt. Josiah Richardson's home in Keene was struck by lightning. A fire ensued which caused considerable damage before it was extinguished. No one was injured. (1,35 8/16/1785)

161. Ship News:

		ENTERED FROM
Sloop *Mary*	Gunnison	Grenada
Schooner *Sally*	Perry	New Brunswick
		CLEARED FOR
Sloop *Adonis*	Marshall	West Indies
Brig *Nancy*	Peirce	Cape Francois
Brig *Astrea*	Salter	West Indies

(1,35 8/16/1785)

162. Ship News:

		ENTERED FROM
Brig *Kitty*	Thwing	St. Domingo
		CLEARED FOR
Schooner *Polly*	Chase	South Carolina

(1,36 8/23/1785)

163. James Haslett has a second hand curricle with complete harness for sale or rent. (1,36 8/23/1785)

164. Died: At Portsmouth, Capt. Alexander Caldwell, 79; a child of Mr. Goode; and a Negro woman, the property of Mrs. Wibird, by drowning. (1,37 8/30/1785)

165. Ship News:

		ENTERED FROM
Brig *Bee*	Fletcher	St. Eustatia
Ship *Hero*	Smallcorn	London
		CLEARED FOR
Schooner *Betsy*	Manning	Martinico
Schooner *Sally*	Perry	St. Peters
Sloop *Mary*	Gunnison	Tobago

(1,37 8/30/1785)

166. Ship News:

		ENTERED FROM
Brig *Dragon*	Oram	Jamaica

		CLEARED FOR
Brig *Susannah*	Mendum	West Indies
Schooner *Tryall*	Lord	West Indies
Brig *Endeavor*	Riley	Tobago
(1,38, 9/6/1785)		

167. Jonathan Moulton notes that there has been a store in Dover since October 1784 by the name of Allen and Moulton. Several persons have bought goods on credit that were delivered from this store by Joseph Allen and William Pitt Moulton. These goods were the property of Jonathan Moulton and payment should be made only to him. Dover, September 1, 1785. (1,38 9/6/1785)

168. George Madden notes that last Thursday evening or Friday morning a poor man lost a bag with 126 skeins of yarn, some tobacco, a hat and a cap. A reward will be paid for return of the bag. Portsmouth, September 6, 1785. (1,38 9/6/1785)

169. Ship News: Last Sunday a brig, Capt. Ritchie, arrived from Glasgow with fifty Scottish emigrants.   They were husbandmen and mechanics. (1,39 9/13/1785)

170. Ship News:		CLEARED FOR
Brig *Polly*	Rice	Martinico
Brig *Irish*	Gimblet	Welsh West Indies
Brig *Kitty*	Thwing	West Indies
(1,39 9/13/1785)		

171. Joseph Allen cautions all persons from adjusting any of the accounts of Allen and Moulton with Jonathan Moulton. Allen claims that Jonathan Moulton has recently broken into the store of Allen and Moulton, belonging to Joseph Allen and William P. Moulton, and taken away goods belonging to the store. Settling with Jonathan Moulton will not satisfy debt to the company of Allen and Moulton. Dover, September 12, 1785. (1,39 9/13/1785)

172. Ebenezer Smith and John Gilman have been appointed commissioners by Joseph Badger, Judge of Probate of Wills, etc. for Strafford County, to settle the claims against the estate of Constantine Sinclear, late of Meredith, yeoman, deceased, represented insolvent. They will conduct business at the home of Lt. George Leighton, innholder in Meredith on the first Monday of the next six months. Meredith, August 25, 1785. (1,39 9/13/1785)

173. John Gilman and George Leighton have been appointed commissioners, by Joseph Badger, Judge of Probate of Wills for Strafford County to settle claims against the estate of Benjamin Swazey, late of Meridith, yeoman, deceased, represented insolvent. They will conduct business at the home of Lt. George Leighton, innholder in Meredith, on the first Monday of the next six months. Meredith, August 25, 1785. (1,39 9/13/1785)

174. Died: At Portsmouth, Mrs. Sarah Fitzgerald, 75.   (1,40 9/20/1785)

175. Ship News:

Ship News:		CLEARED FOR
Ship *Mary Ann*	Seaward	Nantes
Brig *Minerva*	Chamberlain	West Indies

(1,40 9/20/1785)

176. Ship News: A resident of Portsmouth just received a letter dated August 29. It was sent by Capt. Taylor, who sailed from Portsmouth last July, from St. Thomas. He notes that his vessel along with ten brigs and one ship were struck by a hurricane on August 24 while in St. Thomas. Despite Taylor's efforts, his vessel was destroyed. (1,41 9/27/1785)

177. Jonathan Moulton submitted a long letter giving his side of the disagreement with Joseph Allen in trying to settle their accounts in relation to the store in Dover known as Allen & Moulton. After a period on discussion, Moulton and Allen decided to open a store in Dover last November. Mr. Allen agreed to provide 300 pounds the first month and 200 pounds over the winter for operation of the store. His uncle, Daniel

Sarjeant of Boston, would supply the same. Moulton was to provide 500 pounds of stock. The agreement to sell goods was to last two years. In addition, Mr. Moulton joined his son William Pitt Moulton, 18, with Mr. Allen. Mr. Allen did not follow through on his part of the agreement, although Mr. Sarjeant did provide 500 pounds of goods a few month later. Mr. Moulton was so troubled by Mr. Allen's conduct that Moulton had Allen sign a statement at the end of May. Allen's statement said that all the goods in the store and the lumber at the landing were the property of Jonathan Moulton, and that Allen had no stake in this property. His statement was signed in Dover on May 30, 1785. By August, Mr. Moulton restricted Allen from selling stock on credit. In the absence of William Pitt Moulton, Mr. Allen has taken the account books and fled. Hampton, September 19, 1785. (1,41 9/27/1785)

178. James Haslet will carry passengers to nearby towns for reasonable rates in a strong carriage with good horses. (1,41 9/27/1785)

179. Mary Jenkins, wife of Peter Jenkins, of Londonderry, Rockingham County, has eloped from his bed and board and for a long time absented herself from his family. Therefore he forbids all persons from harboring or trusting her on his account and will not pay any debt she may incur. Peter Jenkins, Londonderry, September 12. (1,41 9/27/1785)

180. On July 15, the barn of Brigadier General Nichols of Amherst was struck by lightning and consumed by fire. (1,42 10/4/1785)

181. Died: At Portsmouth, Robert Crow, 23. (1,42 10/4/1785)

182. R. Gerrish would like to purchase a cast iron stove at a reasonable price. (1,42 10/4/1785)

183. The following is a list of letters at the Portsmouth Post Office on October 4, 1785:
•A: John Airs, Saco Falls; John Akin.

•B: Joshua Brackett; Edward Berry; Thomas Brown, Kittery; Samuel Braggs, Dover; John Bevans, Wendell; James Bean, Brentwood; William Blaisdell, Hampton; Joseph Blanchard, Chester; Edward Burrows, Lebanon.

•C: James Condell; Edmund Coffin; Jonathan Chase, Cornish; Dr. John Crane, Dartmouth; James Carruth, Kingston; Jeremiah Cranton; Joshua Cortiss, Hampstead; Samuel Chard; Darby Clancy; Monsieur Coodman,

•D: Mary Davis; D. Forster; Dr. G. Frost; John (5) Fletcher, Thornton;

•F: Robert Fulton, Londonderry;

•G: James Griffin,

•H: John Haggens, Berwick; Samuel Ham; John Hole; Daniel Hood, Wilton; Samuel Huntly, Lempster;

•I: Benjamin Ives, in the care of Samuel Braggs, Dover;

•J: Elijah Jenkins, Berwick; Samuel Jewett, Exeter; Daniel (3) Jones, Hinsdale; Didric Johnson; Samuel Jeffers, Wells; William Jones, New Castle;

•L: William Lovett; Dr. Samuel Langdon, Hampton; Thomas H. Lewis, Kittery;

•M: Duncan McNaughton, to the care of Jonathan Moulton, Hampton; Robert Magill; Mark Mires, Saco; Robert Miller; Elizabeth Moody, Newmarket;

•N: James Nowlen; Betsy Nealson; Benjamin Nason, York;

•O: Matthew O'Brien, Deering; Mr. Oventon,

•P: John Pickering; Samuel Peirson, Exeter; Dr. William Page, Charlestown; Peirce and Dix, Peterborough; Thomas Patterson, Londonderry; Ephraim Perkins, Rochester;

•R: Nathaniel Rogers, Newmarket; Joseph Row; Vere Royse; Matthew Ritche, Old York;

•S: Hugh Sallant, Pelham; Edward (3) Sargeant; Richard Seaman; Nicholas Sewell, York; Jacob Sherburne, Loudon; Thomas Slade; Samuel Smallcorn, Kittery; Samuel Smith, Biddeford; Thomas Smith, to the care of Benjamin Chandler; Thomas Sparhawk, Walpole; Nathaniel Spear; Brigadier General Stark; William Stocker, New Castle; Paul James Sullivan;

•T: Daniel Tenny, Hopkinton;

•W: Meshech Weare, Hampton; Rev. Simeon Williams, Windham; Lucy Wilkins, Amherst.

All addresses are Portsmouth unless otherwise noted. Names are spelled as they appear on the letters. (1,42 10/4/1785)

184. Died: At Portsmouth, John Lewes, 59; Mrs. Ann Breaden, 73; Mrs. Elizabeth Thompson, 36, wife of Samuel Thompson Jr.; a child of Capt. John Pickering; and a child of William Whither. (1,43, 10/11/1785)

185. Jonathan Moulton, noting that he is short of cash to pay unexpected demands on him, asks all those with agreements with him to pay according to those agreements. As cash is in short supply, he will take every merchantable article of produce including beef, pork, cattle, live stock, corn, rye, wheat, flour and peas in lieu of cash. Produce will be collected at Center Harbor, his store in Moultonboro or at Hampton on November 25 and December 25. Hampton, October 10, 1785. (1,43 10/11/1785)

186. The following proprietors in Orford have taxes in part or full delinquent: Theodore Atkinson; Theodore Atkinson Jr.; Mark H. Wentworth; Benning Wentworth; Samuel Wentworth; and Gov. B. Wentworth. Unless full payment is made, property will be auctioned on November 15 at Thomas Leavitt's house in Hampton to cover the unpaid taxes. Jonathan Moulton, collector. Hampton, October 3, 1785. (1,43 10/11/1785)

187. The following proprietors in Moultonboro have taxes in part or full delinquent: John Taylor, John Garland, Thomas Rand, Simon Nudd, Christopher Toppan, Joseph Garland, Josiah Dearborn, Samuel Robinson and John Neal. Unless full payment is made, property will be auctioned on November 15 at Thomas Leavitt's house Jonathan Moulton, collector. Hampton, October 3, 1785. (1,43 10/11/1785)

188. The following proprietors in Piermont have taxes in part or in full delinquent: Mark Hunking Wentworth, Henry Sherburne, Meshech Weare, Capt. Thomas W. Waldron, Peter Gilman, Zebulon Giddinge, Andrew Wiggin, Capt. Timothy Beedle, Major John Wentworth, Theodore Atkinson, and

Theodore Atkinson Jr. Jonathan Moulton, collector. Hampton, October 3, 1785. (1,43 10/11/1785)

189. Ship News: ENTERED FROM
Brig *Abigail*   Peirce   Grenada
Ship *Triton*   Lewis   Boudeaux
(1,44 10/18/1785)

190. Three days of downpour started on October 20. The swollen rivers carried away bridges, mills, stores, vessels, lumber and other objects. At Dover, it carried away thousands of pieces of lumber from a landing and destroyed the store of Major Tibbets including 1000 bushels of salt which were inside. It also almost totally ruined the store of Mr. Horne, but the goods inside were saved. Seven mills and two bridges were also carried away in Dover. The grist mill of Major General Sullivan was carried away from its location in Packer's Falls. (1,46 11/1/1785)

191. Died: At Portsmouth, a child of Daniel Peirce.   (1,46 11/1/1785)

192. Ship News: ENTERED FROM
Schooner *Fly*   Rollings   St. Eustatia
Brig *Mary*   Shores   Cape Francois
(1,46 11/1/1785)

193. The partnership of Goddard and Storer will be dissolved on November 12. All persons are asked to promptly settle their accounts. November 1. (1,46 11/1/1785)

194. N. McIntire has bohea tea, New England rum and other merchandise for sale. (1,46 11/1/1785)

195. Benjamin Dearborn has opened an intelligence office in his home in addition to his auction. At this office one may find information about real estate for sale or rent and information on servant and apprentices for hire. Portsmouth, October 25, 1785. (1,46 11/1/1785)

196.   Nath. Rogers, Josiah Adams and Samuel Baker have been appointed commissioners, by Phillips White, Judge of Probate of Wills, etc. for Rockingham County, to settle claims against the estate of Walter Bryent Jr., late of Newmarket, deceased, represented insolvent. They will conduct business on the first Monday of the next five months at the home of John Shute, innholder, in Newmarket.   Newmarket, October 19.   (1,46 11/1/1785)

197.   A case of merchandise was shipped July 1 from London by Miles Atkinson on board the *Hero*, Capt. Smallcorn. It recently arrived in Portsmouth and is consigned to Joseph Pennice of Wiscasset Point, Sheepscot.   It may be recovered from Jacob Sheafe Jr. by paying charges.   Portsmouth, October 18.   (1,47 11/8/1785)

198.   Ship News:

		ENTERED FROM
Ship *Chalky*	Fernald	Cape Francois
Schooner *Betsy*	Manning	Turks Island
Sloop *Betsy*	Parker	Philadelphia
		CLEARED FOR
Brig *Sophia*	Roberts	Baltimore

(1,47 11/8/1785)

199.   On September 29, 1781, Ebenezer Cleveland, Eleazer Wheelock, and James Wheelock, pretending to be Trustees of Dartmouth College, along with various other persons, extorted John Crissy and John Crissy Jr. by a joint promissary note of hand in the amount of sixty pounds. All persons are cautioned against signing such a note.   Landaff, October 3, 1785.   (1,47 11/8/1785)

200.   Andrew McMillan, Richard Eastman, James Osgood, Stephen Merrill and Abiel Lovejoy, being proprietors and owners of more than one tenth of Conway, ask Thomas Merrill, Proprietors Clerk of Conway, to call a Town Meeting at the meeting house in Conway on December 5 to conduct business of the town. (1,47 11/8/1785)

201. Thomas Merrill calls a town meeting at the time and place noted in item 200. Conway, October 15, 1785. (1,47 11/8/1785)

202. Died: At Portsmouth, William Martin, 39; a child of Phillip Yeaton. (1,47 11/8/1785)

203. Andrew McMillan, Edwards Bucknam and Thomas Merrill have been appointed a committee, by the General Court of New Hampshire to repair from and through Wolfborough to Conway and from Conway to Northumberland at the upper Cohos. This committee advanced twenty two pounds fourteen shillings to pay for repairs on the tract of land granted to Major James Gray. Now unless the owner reemburses Andrew McMillan this sum, the property will be sold at auction. November 8, 1785. (1,47 11/8/1785)

204. Jonathan Moulton, John Moulton, Jonathan Godfree, Simon Jenness, Jonathan Garland and Edward B. Moulton, owners of more than one sixteenth part of Piermont, request Joseph Moulton, Clerk of Proprietors of Piermont to call a Town Meeting at the home of Benjamin Leavitt, innholder in North Hampton, on November 18. This meeting is to conduct town business including a determination if Rev. John Richards should be made minister of Piermont. Hampton, November 1, 1785. (1,48 11/15/1785)

205. Joseph Moulton, Clerk of Proprietors of Piermont, agrees with the meeting requested in item 204. November 1, 1785. (1,48 11/15/1785)

206. Benjamin Dearborn has a few casks of rum for sale. Portsmouth, November 15. (1,48 11/15/1785)

207. Died: At Portsmouth, Miss Martha Chadbourn, 14, daughter of Thomas Chadbourn, of Portsmouth. (1,48 11/15/1785)

208. Ship News: ENTERED FROM
Ship *Elizabeth*   Seaward   Bristol
Brig *Susannah*   Mendum   St. Martins
                                       ARRIVED FROM
Sloop *Two Brothers*   Holman   Tobago
(1,48 11/15/1785)

209. General Sullivan has built a new grist mill and fulling mill on the site of the mills swept away by the recent flood. (1,48 11/15/1785)

210. John Moulton, Proprietor Clerk for Orford states that the Town Meeting for Orford will now be held at Thomas Leavitt's home in Hampton on November 17. Hampton, November 7, 1785. (1,48 11/15/1785)

211. Samuel Storer has a variety of goods, including an assortment of English goods, for sale at his store on Spring Hill next door to the market. (1,48 11/15/1785)

212. Ship News: Yesterday the ship *Free Trader*, Capt. Hopley Yeaton, arrived in 55 days from Harve de Grace. (1,48 11/15/1785)

213. The General Court of New Hampshire passed several acts and resolutions during their last session including the following:
•An act to empower Capt. Carr Leavitt to collect certain taxes in Effingham.
•An act to restore Leonard Whiting to his law.
•An act to empower Jonathan Tilton, of Kensington, to enter a complaint at the Superior Court of Judicature to be held on the fourth Tuesday of April.
•An act to make null and void two Judgements of Court obtained by Margaret Frost against Thomas Pinkham.
•An act to establish a Judgement of the Quatter Sessions of the Peace for Hillsborough County in favor of John Smith and against the selectmen of Peterboro.
•An act to revoke a letter of guardianship granted by the Judge

of Probate of Hillsborough appointing Samuel Foster, guardian of James McClure.

•An Act to give exclusive privilege of keeping a ferry over a certain part of the Connecticut River to Jonathan Mason, of Lyme, his heirs and assigns.

•An Act to restore Noah Cook, of New Ipswich, NH, to his law.

•An Act to empower Samuel Pillsbury to collect certain taxes in the town of Londonderry. (1,49 11/22/1785)

214. Ship News:

		ENTERED FROM
Brig *Endeavor*	Riley	Martinico
Schooner *Tryall*	Lord	St. Eustatia
Ship *Free Trade*	Yeaton	Harve de Grace
		CLEARED FOR
Schooner *Ruth*	Stanford	West Indies

(1,49 11/22/1785)

215. Eliphalet Ladd, of Exeter, and Samuel Hill, of Portsmouth, have bought and are operating a distillary in Portsmouth. They have New England rum as well as European and West India goods for sale. (1,49 11/22/1785)

216. An auction of a variety of goods will be held at Dearborn's auction room on December 1, 1785. Portsmouth, November 21. (1,49 11/22/1785)

217. Died: At Portsmouth, last night, Gen. William Whipple, 55, former Superior Court Judge. (1,50 11/29/1785)

218. Ship News:

		ENTERED FROM
Brig *Jane & Elizabeth*	Fraser	London
		CLEARED FOR
Ship *Atlantic*	Trefethen	W. Indies
Ship *Hero*	Wardrobe	Tobago

(1,50 11/29/1785)

219. A representative of the European community will come to Boston, in July, to sell fur that is a little inferior to beaver. Hatters, merchants and others wishing more details should

contact Isaac Pollack at the Philadelphia Coffee House, in the north end of Boston, or Elias Thomas's near Mr. Hancock's wharf. Boston, October 24. (1,50 11/29/1785)

220.   Alford Butler will sell almanacs of all kinds at his shop, just below Mr. Bowles's. (1,50 11/29/1785)

221.   Mr. Lear will open a school on Monday to teach young ladies reading, writing arithmatic, grammer or geography. He will also teach young gentlemen navigation, geography or use of globes. The school is in the room recently occupied by Mr. Montague. Portsmouth, November 29. (1,50 11/29/1785)

222.   Ship News:

		ENTERED FROM
Brig *Astrea*	Salter	Cape Francois
Brig *Kitty*	Thwing	Cape Francois
Brig *Cooper*	White	Baltimore
		CLEARED FOR
Brig *Nancy*	Frost	West Indies

(1,51 12/6/1785)

223.   Abigail Lewis, Administrix, asks all persons indebted to or with demands on the estate of John Lewis, late of Portsmouth, deceased, to promptly exhibit same. Portsmouth, December 5. (1,51 12/6/1785)

224.   There are a variety of books and some starch for sale at Dearborn's auction room. December 6. (1,51 12/6/1785)

225.   George Doig announces that he continues to operate a painting and gilding business. This includes painting fire buckets at six shillings a pair. (1,51 12/6/1785)

226.   Robert Gerrish is selling his Ladies Almanac for 1786 at his printing office on Congress Street, next door to the Buck and Glove. He also has for sale almanacs by Weatherwise, Low, Bickerstaff and George. (1,51 12/6/1785)

227. Nath. Folsom has new flour and ship bread for sale at his store. Portsmouth, December 4, 1785. (1,51 12/6/1785)

228. Jonathan Moulton, collector, announces that the sale of land of delinquent tax payers in Orford, will be held on December 27 at the home of Thomas Leavitt. December 3. (1,52 12/13/1785)

229. Jonathan Moulton, collector, notifies the delinquent taxpayers of Piermont that their land will be sold on December 27 at the home of Thomas Leavitt, innholder in Hampton. Hampton, December 3. (1,52 12/13/1785)

230. John Moulton, Prop. Clerk, notifies the proprietors of Moultonboro and Orford that their meetings will be held at the home of Thomas Leavitt, innholder in Hampton, on December 27. Hampton, December 3. (1,52 12/13/1785)

231. John Noble, Peter Cowes, William Gardner and John Sparhawk, Selectmen of Portsmouth, ask all persons with accounts open with the town for this year to settle same by the end of the month. Portsmouth, December 8, 1785 (1,52 12/13/1785)

232. Ship News:

		ENTERED FROM
Ship *Lydia*	Tibbets	St. Ubes
		CLEARED FOR
Schooner *Betsy*	Manning	Martinico
Schooner *Dove*	Trefethen	West Indies

(1,52 12/13/1785)

233. C. Storer has for sale drugs, medicine and other merchandise for sale in the store formerly occupied by Goddard & Storer. (1,52 12/13/1785)

234. Samuel Place has just returned from England. There he obtained equipment to execute all types of work on watches and clocks. He will conduct his business in his shop on Buck Street. (1,52 12/13/1785)

235.   Lettice Clagett and Clifton Clagett, administrators, request all persons having demands against the estate of Wiseman Clagett, late of Litchfield, NH, intestate, are requested to promptly present them.   Litchfield, November 1785.   (1,52 12/13/1785)

236.   Died: At Portsmouth, a son, 9, of Major William Gardner. (1,53 12/20/1785)

237.   Ship News:

		ENTERED FROM
Brig *Irish*	Gimblet	Welch Cape Francois
Sloop *Mary*	Gunnison	St. Eustatia
		CLEARED FOR
Brig *Two Sisters*	Jackson	West Indies
Brig *Mary*	Stockell	West Indies
Sloop *Dolphin*	Coffin	West Indies
Schooner *Tryal*	Lord	Martinico

(1,53 12/20/1785)

238.   John Cass advises all taverners and retailers in his district to settle their excise before the meeting of the General Sessions of the Peace, at Exeter, on the fourth Tuesday of December. Exeter, December 15, 1785. (1,53 12/20/1785)

239.   Uniforms for the Militia of New Hampshire are as follows:

	COLORS	FACINGS
General Bellows	white	deep crimson
General Cilley	white	deep blue
General Moulton	white	bright scarlet
General Green	white	green
General Dowe	white	sky blue
Brigade late Hale's	white	black
The Light Horse	green	scarlet
Artillery	blue	scarlet

(1,53 12/20/1785)

240.   The estate in Wolfeboro, formerly owned by Governor Wentworth, is for sale by John and Andrew Cabot of Beverly

and Richard Champney of Portsmouth. Beverly, MA, December 16. (1,53 12/20/1785)

241. Seth Walker, miller, notes that unless people who want grain ground mark their bags as he can not be held responsible for the owner receiving the proper bag. (1,53 12/20/1785)

242. Died: At Portsmouth last Wednesday, Mrs. Hannah Penhallow, comfort of Samuel Penhallow, merchant of Portsmouth; a daughter, 26, of Henry Sherburne; Mrs. Mary Varil, 33. (2,54 12/27/1785)

243. Ship News:

		ENTERED FROM
Brig *Betsey*	Haggens	Port-au-Prince
		CLEARED FOR
Schooner *Fly*	White	West Indies
Brig *Susannah*	Parker	West Indies
Sloop *Fair Play*	York	West Indies

(2,54 12/27/1785)

244. Nath. Shannon, administrator, requests all persons with demands against the estate of Capt. John Lewis, deceased, to exhibit same for settlement. Portsmouth, December 23, 1785. (2,54 12/27/1785)

245. Died: At Portsmouth on December 28, Mark Hunking Wentworth, 76. (2,55 1/3/1786)

246. Ship News:

		CLEARED FOR
Ship *Viscomte d'Arrot*	Palmer	Tobago
Ship *Chalkley*	Thompson	West Indies

(2,55 1/3/1786)

247. Walter Bryent, Administrator, has been granted a license by Phillips White, Judge of Probate of Wills, etc., to sell the personnel estate and two thirds of the real estate of Walter Bryent Jr., late of Newmarket, deceased, represented insolvent. Sale will be held on January 11 on the premises. Newmarket, January 2, 1786. (2,55 1/3/1786)

248. Nath'l Shannon, Administrator announces a public auction to be held January 18 to sell the house recently occupied by and part of the estate of Alice Hight, widow, deceased. The house is located in the north end of Portsmouth near the old ferry ways. It has a garden, barn, small store and water privileges. January 2, 1786. (2,55 1/3/1786)

249. Benjamin Stone, Moses Greenough and Humphrey Noys Jr. have been appointed commissioners, by Phillips White, Judge of Probate for Rockingham County, NH, to examine claims against the estate of Benjamin Kimball, late of Plaistow, deceased, represented insolvent. They will conduct business at the home of Jonathan Kimball Jr. in Plaistow on the first Tuesday of the next sixth months. Plaistow, December 23, 1786. (2,55 1/3/1786)

250. All persons with claims against the estate of Capt. James Hickey, late of Portsmouth, deceased, are requested to present same to Betty Hickey, Executrix. Portsmouth, January 10, 1786. (2,56 1/10/1786)

251. William Bailey notes that since his wife, Mary Bailey, has behaved very indiscreetly, he will not pay any debts that she may incur. Portsmouth, January 7, 1786. (2,56 1/10/1786)

252. Died: At Portsmouth, Mrs. Mary Stoodley, 26, wife of William Stoodley of Newington; the eldest daughter of Rev. Mr. McClintock. (2,56 1/10/1786)

253. Ship News:

		CLEARED FOR
Schooner *William*	Whittemore	Virginia
Brig *Cooper*	White	West Indies

(2,56 1/10/1786)

254. John Waldron, for the committee, announces that the excise for Strafford County will be sold on January 30 at the home of Thomas Shannon, innholder of Dover. Dover, January 9, 1786. (2,56 1/10/1786)

255. Jonathan Moulton announces that there will be a meeting at his home in Hampton on January 26 of the proprietors of Piermont. All proprietors are to settle their tax on or before that date. Hampton, January 7, 1786. (2,56 1/10/1786)

256. Walter Bryent, administrator, announces that the sale of the estate of Walter Bryent Jr., late of Newmarket, deceased, has been delayed until February 2. on the premises. Newmarket, January 11. (2,57 1/17/1786)

257. Ship News:

		CLEARED FOR
Brig *Astrea*	Salter	Hispaniola
Brig *Abigail*	Peirce	West Indies
Sloop *Sally*	Stacy	West Indies
Ship *Triton*	Lewis	West Indies

(2,57 1/17/1786)

258. John Penhallow has flour, bar iron, tar, turpentine and pitch for sale at his store on Long Wharf. (2,57 1/17/1786)

259. Jonathan Moulton, of Hampton, has for sale an oxen, cows and lumber. January 10, 1786. (2,57 1/17/1786)

260. Ship News:

		CLEARED FOR
Brig *Nancy*	Peirce	Cape Francois
Brig *Mary*	Smallcorn	West Indies

(2,58 1/25/1786)

261. John Stavers and John Greenleaf thank their customers and announce that they will continue their stage service. This includes carrying the public mail from Portsmouth to Boston two times a week from the first of November to the first of May and three times a week the rest of the year. The stage will put up at John Staver's tavern in Portsmouth and Col. Dudley Colman's boarding house in Boston. January 1, 1786. (2,59 2/1/1786)

262. Daniel Hill of Newmarket has a genteel close sleigh for sale. (2,59 2/1/1786)

263. Jona. Moulton, collector, reminds the following proprietors of Piermont that their tax of 3 pounds 10 shillings for upkeep of common land in Piermont is delinquent: John Temple, Theodore Atkinson, Richard Wibird, John Downing, Daniel Warner, Joseph Newmarch, Mark H. Wentworth, James Nevin, Theo. Atkinson Jr., Nathaniel Barrell, Henry Sherburne, Meshach Weare, William Parker, Andrew Clarkson, Thomas Waldron, Capt. Howard Henderson, Jonathan Moulton, Christopher Toppan, Peter Gilman, Capt. Zebulon Giddinge, George Frost, Richard Jenness, Benjamin Stevens, Richard Downing, Andrew Wiggin, Samuel Barr, Col. Joseph Smith, John Page, Samuel Emerson, Capt. Jonathan Carleton, Major Joseph Wright, Dr. Jonathan Hale, Col. John Wentworth, Major Joseph Blanchard, Capt. Samuel Greeley, John Goffe, Capt. Ezekiel Worthen, Capt. Jonathan Church, Capt. John McDuffe, Robert Temple, Col. Timothy Beedle, Nathan Whiting, John Fisher, George Jaffrey, Wiseman Clagget, Major John Wentworth, Leverett Hubbart, Thomas Packer, Samuel Wentworth, Peter Livius, John Tufton Mason, George Livius, Dr. Hall Jackson, Robert Auchmuty, Charles Paxton, Daniel Peirce, Gov. Benning Wentworth. Unless these taxes are paid before a meeting at the home of Thomas Leavitt, innholder in Hampton, portions of their land will be sold to cover the taxes. Hampton, January 30. (2,59 2/1/1786)

264. Died: At Portsmouth, John Moffat, 92; Samuel Beck, 87; Mrs. Sarah Salter, 27, daughter of Titus Salter; a child of Samuel Drowne. At Boston, Mrs. Mehetabel Sullivan, comfort of James Sullivan of Boston. (2,59 2/1/1786)

265. Ship News:

		Cleared For
Sloop *Mary*	Gunnison	Tobago
Brig *Endeavor*	Riley	Surinam
Brig *Viscomte D'Arrot*	Miller	Tobago

(2,59 2/1/1786)

266. Ship News:		CLEARED FOR
Brig *Jane & Elizabeth*	Fraser	West Indies
Brig *Carbonear*	Briard	West Indies
Brig *Irish*	Gimblet	Welch West Indies
(2,60 2/8/1786)		

267. Ship News:		CLEARED FOR
Brig *Kitty*	Thwing	West Indies
Brig *Dolphin*	Cutts	West Indies
Brig *Polly*	Rice	West Indies
Sloop *Randolph*	Gardner	West Indies
Schooner *Polly*	Chamberlain	Demerara
(2,61 2/15/1786)		

268. George Doig has a fall back chaise for sale. (2,61 2/15/1786)

269. Charles Waters is establishing a brass founder and caster business on Pitt Street in Portsmouth. (2,61 2/15/1786)

270. Neal McIntire has cherry rum, cognac, tar, pitch and turpentine for sale. (2,63 3/1/1786)

271. On February 14, the 10 year old daughter of Joseph Tucker, suffer a terrible accident. She was carrying a lighted pitch torch which set fire to flax and herbs. The daughter could not escape the fire and died in the blaze. (2,63 3/1/1786)

272. Joseph Bass has an assortment of garden seeds for sale at his store in Portsmouth. (2,63 3/1/1786)

273. As Nathaniel Sparhawk will be sailing to Europe soon, he requests that those having accounts with him settle them promptly. He also is selling some household furniture at public auction on March 15. Portsmouth, February 28, 1786. (2/63 3/1/1786)

274. John Sullivan resigns as Major General of the New Hampshire Militia in order that he can exert his energy to the

position of Attorney General which he was just appointed. Portsmouth, February 28, 1786. (2/64 3/8/1786)

275.   James MacGregore and Jonathan Cass have purchased the excise on spiritous liquor in Rockingham County from October 1, 1785 to October 1, 1786. Therefore all taverners and retailers are requested to pay the first two quarters tax on April 1 at the home of Col. Brewster of Henry Sherburne in Portsmouth. Portsmouth, March 2, 1786. (2,64 3/8/1786)

276.   A man of indisputable character is wanted to live on and tend a farm about three miles from Portsmouth. If interested contact R. Gerrish. (2,64 3/8/1786)

277.   Last November 15 in Salem, Richard Squire and John Matthews were convicted of robbery and a felony on the high seas. Last Saturday they were sentenced to ten years of hard labor. Boston March 13. (2,65 3/15/1786)

278.   During the last session of the General Court of New Hampshire, many acts and resolutions were passed including the following:
•Edwards Buckman, of Lancaster, Grafton County, and his heirs were vested exclusive privilege to keep a ferry on the Connecticut River.
•The Superior Court of Judicature was empowered to render judgement for damages and costs in an action brought to the court by Zebulon Marst against Edward Hilton.
•It was resolved that the commissioners to the estate of Breed Batchelder receive and consider the claim of Oliver Wright. They are to allow the claim if it proves just.
•Confirmed the title of certain lands to Barnabas Barker.
•Granted the privilege of a ferry to Samuel Bayley.
•Granted the privilege of a ferry to Benjamin Bellows.
•Granted the privilege of a ferry to Joseph Kimball.
•Restored the right of Henry Kennison to certain land in Barnstead.
•Restored Hugh Tallant to law.
•Vested ferry right to Moses Chase,

•Vacated the proceedings on an execution against Joseph Kelly.
•Annulled and voided a judgement of court obtained by Ebenezer Torrey, David Larnard and Abel Larnard.
•Discounted Israel Morey's execution.
•Restored John Fisher's property in New Hampshire.
•Restored John Young to his law.
•Restored to Benjamin Cummings his share of real estate from his late father.
•Granted the privilege of a ferry to Thomas Burnsid.
•Granted the privilege of a ferry to Micah Reed.
•Amended and relieved against a mistake made in a levy on the execution in favor of Jonathan Warner against William Reeves and others.
•Granted the privilege of a ferry to Solomon Robbins.
•Restored John Pickering Jr. to his land. (2,65 3/15/1786)

279. A vote was taken at the Town Meeting in Concord on March 7, for state President and Senator. Those receiving votes listed in descending order are as follows:

PRESIDENT

John Langdon   George Atkinson
John Sullivan

SENATOR

John McClary   Nathaniel Peabody
Joseph Gilman   Joshua Wentworth
Peter Green   John Bell.

(2,65 3/15/1786)

280. Ship News: ENTERED FROM
Schooner *Dove*   Trefethren   St. Eustatia
                                CLEARED FOR
Brig *Three Brothers* Sherburne   West Indies
(2,65 3/15/1786)

281. Samuel Bean who has rider Post from Boston to New Hampshire for several years has been appointed to ride Post

from Portsmouth to Amherst via Greenland, Stratham, Exeter, Kingston, Hawke, Sandown, Chester, Londonderry, Litchfield, and Merrimac. He will also deliver the *New Hampshire Mercury*. (2,65 3/15/1786)

282. Susanna Spafford writes an open letter to the public in response to a letter written by John Spafford, her husband, in the February 6, 1786 edition of the *New Hampshire Gazette*. She claims to be an obedient, loving, chaste and kind wife since their marriage. About three months offered a hired man dinner. Her husband was so jealous that he physically abused her. His claims of her having a do with several men is false. Since living in Salem, he has beaten her so bad that she was black and blue for several weeks. (2,65 3/15/1786)

283. Samuel Cate notes that David Gardner, tailor, of Portsmouth, has sundry notes signed by Cate which have already been paid. Cate has a right of land in Cohass for sale. (2,65 3/15/1786)

284. Died: At Portsmouth, Mrs. Deborah Mills, widow of the late Capt. Luke Mills, of Portsmouth. (2,66 3/22/1786)

285. Ship News:
Schooner *Tryall*   Lord   ENTERED FROM   St. Eustatia
(2,66 3/22/1786)

286. Results of voting for officials at the Town Meeting in Portsmouth on March 25 are as follows:
State Representatives — John Langdon, John Pickering, John Sparhawk
Town Clerk — John Evans
Selectmen — John Sparhawk, John Nobles, Capt. Peter Cowes, Nathaniel Folsom, William Gardner
Assessors — George Gains, Col. Samuel Sherburne, Dr. A. R. Cutter, Jeremiah Libbey, Samuel Sherburne (Plains)
Overseers of the Poor — George Atkinson, Joshua Wentworth,

Daniel Rindge, Dr. A. R. Cutter, Dr. John Jackson, Richard Champney, Jacob Sheafe Jr., Thomas Sheafe, Benjamin Dearborn

Auditors — John Sherburne, John Parker, Joshua Wentworth

Agents — Samuel Penhallow, Samuel Cutts

Keeper of the Magazine — Jeremiah Libbey

Attornies — John Pickering, Oliver Whipple

Fire Wards — John Langdon, Woodbury Langdon, John Parker, Capt. George Wentworth, Joshua Wentworth, Nathaniel Folsom, Nathaniel Treadwell, Jacob Sheafe Jr., John Noble, Jeremiah Libbey, Capt. Ephraim Ham, Capt. Ichabod Nichols, James Sheafe,

Constables — Clement March, George Ham Jr., Thomas Chadbourne, William Vaughan

Lot Layers — Samuel Hale, William Hart, Nathaniel Adams

Fence Viewers — Samuel Sherburne (Plains), Joseph Tucker, Capt. Samuel Hall, Abraham Elliot, William Ham, Walter Akerman

Searchers and Sealers of Leather — George Dame, Nathaniel Jackson, Perkins Ayers

Sealer of Weights and Measures — Daniel Lunt

To inquire who killed deer out of season — Capt. George Wentworth

Cullers and Packers of Fish — Joseph Walton, George Howe, George Hull, John Pitman

Pound Keeper — John Dennett

Surveyors of Boards and Measurers of Timber — Samuel Jackson, Samuel Hutchings, William Wilson, John Beck, Moses Noble

Measurers of wood by land and water — John Beck, William Yeaton, Shackford Seaward, Samuel Beck, Ephraim Dennett, Henry Sherburne, John Melcher, William Moses

Corders of Wood — Joseph Benson, William Walden, Thomas Priest, Richard Peverly, Samuel Jones, George Walden

Hog Reeves — William Walden, Charles Waters, Samuel Ham (Plains), Joseph Wincoll

(2,67 3/29/1786)

287. Ship News: ENTERED FROM
Sloop *Fair Play*   York   St. Lucia
Sloop *Adventure*   Scott   Baltimore
                                            CLEARED FOR
Brig *Betsy*   Haggens   West Indies
(2,67 3/29/1786)

288. John Noble, Peter Cowes, Nath'l Folsom and Wm. Gardner, selectmen for Portsmouth, that as directed by the state treasurer, are requiring all residents to make exact inventories of their rateable polls and estates so that proper taxes may be applied. Portsmouth, March 28, 1786. (2,67 3/29/1786)

289. Thomas W. Weare and Redford Weare, executors to the estate of Meshech Weare, late of Hampton Falls, deceased, are requested to promptly present all claims against the estate. (2,67 3/29/1786)

290. Gilbert Horney has recently imported English goods for sale at his shop opposite Mr. Staver's Tavern. Portsmouth, March 28, 1786. (2,67 3/29/1789)

291. Jonathan Moulton, of Hampton, and George Libbey, of Greenland, have clover seed for sale. Hampton, March 29, 1786. (2,67 3/29/1786)

292. Died: At Portsmouth, Joseph Gerrish, 32, of Portsmouth, drowned. (2,68 4/5/1786)

293. Ship News: ENTERED FROM
Sloop *Sally*   Stacy   St. Eustatia
Brig *Nancy*   Frost   Cape Francois
Ship *Atlantic*   Trefethen   Port-au-Prince
Brig *Cooper*   White   Cape Francois
(2,68 4/5/1786)

294. Ship News: His Most Christian Majestry's Packet, built in New Hampshire, will soon sail for New York and then for

l'Orient under the command of the Chevalier D'Aboville. For freight or passage apply to M. Ducher. (2,68 4/5/1786)

295. Ship News: A brig from Portsmouth, Capt. Samuel Pearce, bound here from the West Indies, was washed ashore just south of Plymouth Harbor in a snow storm. The cargo will be saved and it is believed that the vessel can be refloated. (2,69 4/12/1786)

296. Ship News:

		CLEARED FOR
Brig *Dispatch*	Tibbets	West Indies
Brig *Lydia*	Tibbets	West Indies

(2,69 4/12/1786)

297. Ship News: The sloop *Sally*, moored at the north end of town, will sail for Philadelphia next week. Contact Robert Parker for passage or cargo. (2,69 4/12/1786)

298. George Doig has a fall back chaise for sale. (2,69 4/12/1786)

299. Died: At Portsmouth at Col. Brewster's, Nero, 75, late king of the Africans in Portsmouth. (2,70 4/19/1786)

300. Ship News:

		ENTERED FROM
Sloop *Dolphin*	Coffin	St. Eustatia

(2,70 4/19/1786)

301. Ichabod Nichols has St. Ubes salt for sale at his store in the south end. Portsmouth, April 17, 1786. (2,70 4/19/1786)

302. Died: At Portsmouth, Mrs. Olive Green, 22. (2,71 4/26/1786)

303. Ship News:

		CLEARED FOR
Brig *Polly*	Briard	West Indies
Schooner *Dove*	Trefethen	West Indies

(2,71 4/26/1786)

304. William Gardner, John Parker and Joshua Brackett, appointed Commissioners to examine claims against the estate of Tobias Lear, late of Portsmouth, mariner, deceased, represented insolvent, will conduct their business on the last Tuesday of the next six months at the home of William Brewster in Portsmouth. Portsmouth, April 26. (2,71 4/26/1786)

305. Peter Cowes, John Sparhawk, John Noble, Nath'l Folsom and W. Gardner, Overseers of the Poor, have uncovered an illegal practice. Some shopkeepers are buying merchandise at low prices which they know to be stolen. Unless this practice stops, their names will be exposed and they will be prosecuted according to law. Portsmouth, April 24, 1786. (2,71 4/26/1786)

306. Ship News:

		ENTERED FROM
Brig *Susannah*	Parker	Turks Island
Brig *Astrea*	Salter	Port-au-Prince
Schooner *Fly*	Twombly	Demerara
		CLEARED FOR
Sloop *Sally*	Smith	Philadelphia

(2,72 5/3/1786)

307. Jonathan Moulton, collector, announces that the sale of delinquent proprietors' common and undivided land in Piermont will be held May 8 at the home of Thomas Leavitt. Property will be sold unless accounts are paid in full. Hampton, May 1, 1786. (2,72 5/3/1786)

308. Jonathan Cass, excise master, requests that all persons in his district settle their excise for 1785. Exeter, April 24, 1786. (2,72 5/3/1786)

309. Died: At Portsmouth, Capt. John Dennet, 70, leaving a widow and eight children. (2,73 5/10/1786)

310. Ship News:

		ENTERED FROM
Schooner *Four Brothers*	Sellars	West Indies
Ship *Atlantic*	Trefethen	West Indies
Schooner *Union*	Salter	West Indies

Ship News (continued):   ENTERED FROM
Schooner *Betsy*   Manning   St. Peters
Brig *Nancy*   Frost   West Indies
(2,73 5/10/1786)

311. Died: At Portsmouth, Supply Boyd, 14, son of George Boyd of Portsmouth. (2,73 5/10/1786)

312. Ship News: ENTERED FROM
Brig *Abigail*   Peirce   St. Eustatia
Schooner *Polly*   Chamberlain   Surinam
(2,74 5/17/1786)

313. A meeting of the heirs of Samuel Allen, and their assigns was held at the home of James Thurston, innholder in Exeter, NH on September 20, 1785. They chose John Sullivan, Nathaniel Peabody, Peter Green, Capt. Leonard Whiting and Samuel Lauchlan as agents with full power in behalf of this propriety. Another meeting of these proprietors was held at the home of widow Sarah Webster, innholder in Chester on January 25, 1786. There they voted that the agents give quit claim deeds to those who provide evidence of buying property in the Allen claim. Attested to by Peter Green, Prop'rs Clerk. (2,74 5/17/1786)

314. John Sullivan of Durham, Nathaniel Peabody of Atkinson and Peter Green of Concord, acting as the majority of the agents of the heirs and assigns of the estate of Samuel Allen deceased, do quit claim all property bought within the property of Samuel Allen. This was signed before John Dudley and Abiel Foster on April 27, 1786. (2,74 5/17/1786)

315. John Sullivan, writing for himself and the heirs and assigns of Samuel Allen, gives some background of the ownership problems that existed in items 313 and 314. The state of New Hampshire owes its origin to a grant to Capt. John Mason in 1629, that was confirmed in 1635. He was conveyed all land that were enclosed within the following boundaries: From the mouth of the Piscataqua River to the headwater of the same, thence northwesterly for 60 miles and another line

running up the Merrimac River, then westerly 60 miles, then by a line connecting the end of the first two lines. This land was passed on to Mason's sons, John and Robert. In 1691 they sold this property to Samuel Allen for 2750 pounds shilling. Allen took possession of the land and it was passed on to Samuel Allen's son Thomas when Samuel died. In 1747, a several people purchased for 750 pounds, from a descendent of Capt. Mason, his rights within the above mentioned land. They moved in and took possession of such land, even though it was widely known that there was no legal basis to this claim. These people claimed the title of proprietors of the Mason grant and made grants to several townships while reserving the best land for themselves. The true owners lost power and were forced to Massachusetts and Rhode Island to earn a living. Just about three years ago they gained enough wealth to try and regain their rights through the courts. At that time they only wanted to regain that property that had not been improved or developed. This matter will be brought up at the next General Assembly. Durham, May 8. 1786. (2,74 5/17/1786)

316. George Doig has water colors and good linseed oil for sale. (2,74 5/17/1786)

317. Died: At Portsmouth, Mrs. Elizabeth Abbot, 65. (2,75 5/24/1786)

318. Ship News:

		ENTERED FROM
Brig *Polly*	Rice	Martinico
Brig *Mary*	Smallcorn	Cape Francois
Brig *Irish*	Gimblet	Welsh Martinico
Ship *Hero*	Wardrobe	Tobago
		CLEARED FOR
Schooner *Fly*	Twombly	West Indies

(2,75 5/24/1786)

319. The President of New Hampshire, on the advice of Council, has approved the recommendation of the legislature to name the following as Surveyors of Lumber:
Portsmouth — John Beck, Samuel Briard, Samuel Hutchins.

Dover — Benjamin Peirce, Thomas Shannon, David Folsom.
Exeter — Simeon Ladd, James Rundlett, Ephraim Robinson, Nathaniel Giddinge Jr.
Durham — John Smith, III, Samuel Yeaton.
Newmarket — Walter Bryent, William Odiorne.
Somersworth — John Rollins.
Attested to by E. Thompson, Sec'y. (2,75 5/24/1786)

320. Nath'l Rogers, Josiah Adams, and Samuel Baker, commissioners to examine the claims against the estate of Walter Bryent Jr, deceased, represented insolvent, will conduct business at the home of John Shute, innholder in Newmarket on the first Tuesday of the next five months. Newmarket, May 8, 1786. (2,75 5/24/1786)

321. Alexander Bruce, boot and shoe maker, advises that he has moved his business from Boston to Portsmouth. He is located on Buck Street (formerly Queen St.) where he makes fine men's footwear. Portsmouth, May 18, 1786. (2,75 5/24/1786)

322. Died: At Portsmouth, a child of Mr. Neal. (2,76 5/31/1786)

323. Ship News:

		ENTERED FROM
Brig *Endeavor*	Riley	Martinico
		CLEARED FOR
Brig *Astrea*	Salter	Hispaniola
Schooner *Success*	Fernald	West Indies
Sloop *Mary*	Fernald	West Indies
Brig *Susannah*	Parker	West Indies
Brig *Polly*	Rice	West Indies
Brig *Abigail*	Pierce	West Indies
Brig *Mary*	Shores	West Indies
Schooner *Nancy*	Brown	West Indies

(2,76 5/31/1786)

324. John Langdon, President of New Hampshire, proclaims the General Court of New Hampshire dissolved. Signed May 31, 1786 and attested to by E. Thompson, Sec'y. (2,76 5/31/1786)

325. R. Gerrish is taking subscriptions for Pike's System of Arithmetic. (2,76 5/31/1786)

326. Charles Waters, brass founder and caster, has established a founding and casting business on Pitt Street, Portsmouth. (2,76 5/31/1786)

327. Ship News:

		ENTERED FROM
Sloop *Randolph*	Gardner	Trinidad
Brig *Kitty*	Thwing	St. Eustatia
Brig *Two Sisters*	Jackson	Baltimore
Schooner *Polly*	Burke	Philadelphia
Sloop *Sally*	Smith	Philadelphia
		CLEARED FOR
Brig *Polly*	Rice	West Indies
Ship *Hero*	Wardrobe	West Indies
Brig *Irish*	Gimblet	Welch West Indies
Brig *Mary*	Pearse	West Indies
Brig *Endeavor*	Riley	West Indies

(2,77 6/7/1786)

328. Aaron Hill has for sale recently arrived form London, a few piece goods as well as calicos and Irish Linens at his shop opposite the state house. (2,77 6/7/1786)

329. John Sullivan has been selected President of New Hampshire by the majority of voters. (2,78 6/14/1786)

330. Died: At Portsmouth, a son of Daniel Gookins; and a child of John Ham. (2,78 6/14/1786)

331. All persons with claims against the estate of Jonathan Shaw, of Brentwood, deceased, are requested to present these claims to Samuel Cram, Administrator, for settlement. Brentwood, May 30, 1786. (2,78 6/14/1786)

332.   A list of state SENATORS:
ROCKINGHAM COUNTY

John McClary	Joseph Gilman
George Atkinson	Joshua Wentworth
John Bell	

STRAFFORD COUNTY

Otis Baker	John McDuffe

HILLSBOROUGH COUNTY

Matthew Thornton	Ebenezer Webster

CHESHIRE COUNTY

John Bellows	Amos Sheppard

GRAFTON COUNTY

Elisha Payne

Counsellors to His Excellency—Joshua Wentworth, Amos Sheppard, Christopher Toppan, Robert Means, Moses Dowe

Speaker of the House of Representatives—John Langdon
Clerk of the House—John Calfe
Secretary—Joseph Pearson
Treasurer—John Taylor Gilman
Commissary General—Supply Clap
(2,79 6/21/1786)

333.   Joseph Pearson, Sec'y, attests that Stephen Barker, of Andover, MA, yeoman, has petitioned the General Court of New Hampshire. He states that on the last day of March 1782, Capt. Kean took action against him for a large sum of money. This was brought before the Inferior Court of Common Pleas in Portsmouth on the first Tuesday of May 1782.   For various reasons, the case was not resolved, so Barker now seeks action before the General Court.   Concord, June 16, 1786.   (2,79 6/21/1786)

334.   All persons with demands on the estate of James Bean, late of Brentwood, deceased, are requested to present same to Elisha Bean, executor. He will conduct business at the home of Richard Bean, of Brentwood, on the last Monday of the next four months. Kingston, June 18, 1786. (2,79 6/21/1786)

335. All persons with demands on the estate of Benjamin Sanborn Jr., late of Salisbury, husbandman, deceased, represented insolvent, are requested to present same to Eben. Webster or Joseph Bean, Commissioners. They will conduct business at the home of Ebenezer Webster, of Salisbury on the first Tuesday of the next six months. Salisbury, June 16, 1786. (2,79 6/21/1786)

336. James Haslett will buy sheep and lamb skins for cash at the sign of the buck and glove. Portsmouth, June 18, 1786. (2,79 6/21/1786)

337. All persons with demands on the estate of Jonathan Taylor, late of Canterbury, deceased, are requested to present same to Jeremiah Clough, Obadiah Hall and Samuel Gerrish, Commissioners appointed by Philips White, Judge of Probate of Rockingham County. They will conduct business at the home of Jeremiah Clough Jr. in Canterbury on the last Wednesday of the next four months. Canterbury, June 7, 1786. (2,79 6/21/1786)

338. A list of the members of the NEW HAMPSHIRE HOUSE OF REPRESENTATIVES:

Portsmouth	John Langdon, Speaker*
	John Pickering
	John Sparhawk
Exeter	Ephraim Robinson*
Londonderry	Col. Daniel Runnels*
	Archibald McMurphy
Chester	Capt. John Underhill*
Rye	Samuel Jenness
North Hampton	Col. Moses Leavitt
Hampton	Christopher Toppan
Hampton Falls &	
Seabrook	Ensign Elisha Brown*
Stratham	Col. Mark Wiggin
Kensington	Moses Shaw
South Hampton &	
East Kingston	Joseph Merrill*

(NEW HAMPSHIRE HOUSE OF REPRESENTATIVES)

Epping	Jonathan Elliot*
Nottingham	Lt. John Gile*
Deerfield	Moses Bernard
Chichester &	
Pittsfield	John Cram*
Canterbury &	
Northfield	Asa Foster*
Pembroke	Samuel Daniels*
Candia	Col. Nathaniel Emerson
Hawke & Sundown	Moses Hook*
Atkinson & Plaistow	Col. J. Welch
Salem	Capt. Amos Dow*
Windham	James Batten
Pelham	James Gibson*
Dover	Col. John Waldron
Somersworth	John Rawlings*
Rochester	James Knowles
Barrington	Maj. Samuel Hale*
Gilmanton	Col. Joseph Badger
Lee	Dr. James Brackett
Sandwich & Tamworth	Daniel Bedee*
Moultonboro, Tuftonboro, Wolfeboro &	
Ossipee Gore	Capt. Nathaniel Ambrose*
Barnstead &	
New Durham	Jonathan Chasly*
Wakefield, Middleton &	
Effingham	Simeon Dearborn*
Nottingham West	Samuel Marsh
Dunstable	Col. Noah Lovell*
Merrimac	Capt. William Barron*
Bedford	Stephen Dole*
Goffstown	Lt. William Page*
Hollis	Daniel Emerson
Amherst	Maj. Robert Means
Raby & Mason	Benjamin Mann*
New Ipswich	Dr. John Preston*
Wilton	Col. Philip Putnam
Lyndeboro	Levi Spaulding

(NEW HAMPSHIRE HOUSE OF REPRESENTATIVES)

Temple & Peterborough Slip	Francis Cragin
Peterborough & Society Land	Capt. Samuel Cunningham*
Hancock, Antrim & Deering	John Duncan
Henniker & Hillsboro	Maj. Robert Wallace
Weare	Capt. George Hadley
Hopkinton	Aaron Greeley*
Dunbarton & Bow	James Clements*
Salisbury	Capt. Robert Smith
Boscawen	George Jackman
Fisherfield, Sutton & Warner	Zephaniel Clark*
Charlestown	John Hubbard*
Keene	Capt. Jeremiah Stiles*
Swanzey	Abraham Randall*
Richmond	Jonathan Gaskill
Jaffrey	John Gilmore
Winchester	Capt. Daniel Ashley*
Westmoreland	Capt. Samuel Works
Chesterfield	Moses Smith*
Claremount	Sanford Kingsbury*
Cornish & Grantham	Dudley Chase*
Newport & Craydon	Jeremiah Jenks
Acworth, Lempster & Marlow	Silas Mack*
Surry & Gilsom	Samuel Holmes
Stoddard & Washington	Capt. Jacob Copland
Dublin & Packersfield	Stephen Ames*
Fitzwilliam	Samuel Kendall
Plainfield	Maj. Joseph Kimbell
Holderness, Campton, Thorton, Lincoln & Franconia	Hercules Mooney*
Plymouth, Rumney & Wentworth	Capt. Absalom Peters*

(NEW HAMPSHIRE HOUSE OF REPRESENTATIVES)
    New Chester, Alexandria &
        Cockermouth   Joshua Tolford*
    Enfield, Canaan, Cardigan, Dorchester &
        Grafton   Jesse Johnson*
    Hanover   Capt. Aaron Storrs*
    Lebanon   Maj. Edmund Freeman*
    Lyme & Orford   Joseph Skinner*
    Haverhill, Piermont, Warren, &
        Coventry   Moses Dow
    Bath, Lyman, Landaff, Concord &
        Dalton   Maj. John Young
* indicates man not a representative last session.
(2,80 6/28/1786)

339. The General Court has selected John Langdon, Pierce Long and John Sparhawk to represent New Hampshire in the U.S. Congress for the next year. (2,80 6/28/1786)

340. Died: At Portsmouth, Samuel Card, 19. (2,80 6/28/1786)

341. Ship News: ENTERED FROM
Schooner *Dove*   Trefethren   Martinico
                                       CLEARED FOR
Sloop *Sally*   Smith   Philadelphia
(2,80 6/28/1786)

342. A large chestnut colored horse was stolen from William Brewster's pasture on June 25. A $10 reward will be paid for its return. Portsmouth, June 27. (2,80 6/28/1786)

343. All persons with demands on the estate of Richard Kitson, late of Portsmouth, mariner, deceased, represented insolvent, are requested to present same to Jeremiah Libbey, John Fernald or John Evans, commissioners. They will conduct business at the post office on the last Tuesday of the next six months. Portsmouth, June 22, 1786. (2,80 6/28/1786)

344. Ship News:

		ENTERED FROM
Brig *Viscomte de Arrot*	Miller	Tobago
Brig *Carbonear*	Briard	Port-au-Prince
		CLEARED FOR
Brig *Two Sisters*	Jackson	Guadaloupe

(2,81 7/5/1786)

345. Thirty four masts, eight bowsprits and eighty yards will be sold at public vendue on July 25 at Portsmouth. For details contact M. Toscan in Boston or M. Ducher in Portsmouth. Portsmouth, July 1, 1786. (2,81 7/5/1786)

346. Samuel Bean has been appointed by the General Court to ride post through the following towns: Portsmouth, Exeter, Nottingham, Concord, Plymouth, Haverhill, Dartmouth, Hanover, Charlestown, Keene, Amherst, Londonderry, Chester and Kingston. Portsmouth, June 21, 1786. (2,81 7/5/1786)

347. R. Gerrish is taking subscriptions at his office on Congress St. for Pike's System of Arithmetic. (2,81 7/5/1786)

348. Alexander Bruce, boot and shoe maker, is opening a shop on Buck Street. (2,81 7/5/1786)

349. The two story home of Capt. Wiswell, in Arundel, was struck by lightning on the evening of June 8. The house suffered some damage. No one was seriously injured. (2,82 7/12/1786)

350. Ship News:

		CLEARED FOR
Sloop *Randolph*	Gardner	West Indies
Schooner *Polly*	Chase	South Carolina

(2,82 7/12/1786)

351. The newly built ship *Hope*, Thomas Thompson, will sail for Poole or a port near the Isle of White by August 1. For passage or cargo apply to Thomas or Jacob Sheafe. (2,82 7/12/1786)

352. Ship News:		ENTERED FROM
Sloop *Endeavor*	York	St. Eustatia
Schooner *Four Brothers*	Sellers	Martinico
Brig *Dispatch*	Tibbets	St. Lucia
Sloop *Mary*	Gunnison	Tobago
Brig *Three Brothers*	Sherburne	Turks Island

(2,84 7/19/1786)

353. The privilege of the ferry in Portsmouth with boats and equipment will be sold at public vendue at the home of Col. William Brewster on July 31. Portsmouth, July 13.
(2,84 7/19/1786)

354. A pale red, four year old cow strayed or was stolen from the farm of Madam Langdon about ten days ago. A reward will be paid for its return. Portsmouth, July 14, 1786.
(2,84 7/19/1786)

355. Samuel Dearborn has been appointed by the General Court of New Hampshire to ride post between the following towns: Portsmouth, Newmarket, Durham, Dover, Rochester, Wakefield, Ossipee Gore, Tamworth, Sandwich, Moultonboro, Center Harbor, Meredith, Gilmanton, Barnstead and Barrington. Portsmouth, July 18, 1786. (2,85 7/26/1786)

356. Joseph Badger, 18, indented servant, formerly of Newmarket ran away from Henry Sherburne on July 24. A one shilling reward is offered for Badger's return. Portsmouth, July 26, 1786. (2,85 7/26/1786)

357. Ship News:		ENTERED FROM
Schooner *Polly*	Briard	Martinico
Brig *Sophia*	Roberts	l'Orient
Sloop *Sally*	Smith	Philadelphia
		CLEARED FOR
Sloop *Dolphin*	Coffin	St. Peters
Brig *Kitty*	Thwing	West Indies

(2,86 8/2/1786)

358. Daniel Sewall, vendue master, will hold a public vendue on August 17 at the home of Dr. Daniel Pierce, in Kittery, to sell non-resident deliquent proprietors' land in Shapleigh, York County, unless taxes are paid before that date. York, July 8, 1786. (2,86 8/2/1786)

359. R. Champney will pay cash for flax seed at the store opposite the post office. Portsmouth, August 2, 1786. (2,86 8/2/1786)

360. All persons will demands on the estate of Capt. John Dennett, deceased, are to present claims to Phebe Dennett and John Dennett, Executors, for prompt payment. (2,86 8/2/1786)

361. George S. Homans has resumed his tailor business at his shop opposite Dr. Hall Jackson's, on Pitt Street. (2,86 8/2/1786)

362. James Colby, 18, an apprentice boy, about six feet tall with light complexion, ran away from Jonathan Eastman on July 23. A half a penny reward is offered for his return. Hampstead, July 25, 1786. (2,86 8/2/1786)

363. Died: At Portsmouth, Thomas Hart, 22, son of Capt. George Hart of Portsmouth. (2,87 8/9/1786)

364. Ship News:

		CLEARED FROM
Sloop *Mary*	Gunnison	West Indies
Ship *Hope*	Thompson	Poole
Schooner *Betsey*	Salter	Martinico
Sloop *Endeavor*	York	West Indies

(2,87 8/9/1786)

365. Ship News: On August 2, the ship *Mary Ann*, Capt. Joseph Seaward, sixty days out of Nantz en route Portsmouth, ran aground on Long Island near Mount Desert. It is believed that the hull and most of the cargo will be lost. (2,88 8/9/1786)

366. Ship News:

		ENTERED FROM
Sloop *Friendship*	Fuller	New York

Brig *Irish Gimblet*	Turner	Guadaloupe
		CLEARED FOR
Brig *Dauphin*	Cutts	West Indies
(2,88 8/16/1786)		

367. J. Pearson, Sec'y, attests that a petition has been presented to the General Court of New Hampshire by Sarson Belcher of Boston, MA. on behalf of himself and the proprietors and land owners in Peterborough. It states that in June 1738 a grant of the tract which is now Peterborough was made to certain people by the General Court of Massachusetts Bay. This empowered Jonathan Prescott to call a meeting of proprietors to lay out and settle Peterborough. The proprietors of the Mason patent, in 1748, quitted to the grantees under Massachusetts their right to this land. The proprietors purchased a book and recorded land transactions. Since the master record book of the General Court of Massachusetts from 1737 to 1746 was consumed in a fire, it is requested that the proprietors' book be substituted as the official book. (2,88 8/16/1786)

368. A wide variety of goods will be sold at Dearborn's auction room tomorrow. August 16, 1786. (2,88 8/16/1786)

369. Edmund H. Quincy will buy flax seed with cash, English or West India goods. (2,88 8/16/1786)

370. Joshua Pike, collector, announces a public vendue will be held the North Meeting House on August 28 to sell pews that have taxes overdue for 1785. The owners of these pews are Capt. John Ayers, Jeremiah Libbey, Eleazer Russell, James Sheafe, Charles Roberts and the heirs of Widow Mayo. Portsmouth, August 15, 1786. (2,88 8/16/1786)

371. Joseph Pearson, Sec'y, attests that a petition has been presented to the General Court by the selectmen of Unity. It notes that a warrant was issued by the selectmen to Caleb Huntoon, constable, to warn Dearborn Sweat and others to depart Unity. This petition was mislaid and thus not entered into the files of the General Sessions of Cheshire County. It is

requested that this filing error be corrected. Exeter, August 15, 1786. (2,88 8/16/1786)

372. Daniel Brainard, a Justice of the Peace for Grafton County, grants the request of owners of more than one sixteenth of the land of Romney to hold a meeting at the home of Maj. Alexander Craig, of Romney on September 4. The purpose of the meeting is to conduct town business. Romney, August 2, 1786. (2,88 8/16/1786)

373. Ship News:

		ENTERED FROM
Schooner *Fly*	Paul	St. Martins
Schooner *Tryal*	Lang	St. Bartholomew
Schooner *Success*	Fernald	Martinico
Brig *Abigail*	Pierce	Martinico
Ship *Atlantic*	Trefethen	Guadaloupe
Schooner *Fortune*	Couliard	Halifax
		CLEARED FOR
Brig *Cooper*	Sellars	West Indies

(2,89 8/23/1786)

374. Jonathan Moulton of Hampton notes that he has expended much money to encourage the settlement of waste lands in New Hampshire. However, his plans are coming to fruition slower than expected and a large burden of taxes on his property has been placed on him. This makes it necessary for him to seek prompt payment of debts owed to him. As cash is in short supply he will also take all kinds of produce in payment at his homes in Orford and Piermont or at his store in Center Harbor. He advises his creditors that he has a plentiful estate including improved farms as well as unimproved land in Moultonboro, New Hampton, Tamworth, Orford, Piermont, Bath Gunthwait, Eaton, Burton, Chatham and other towns. He is willing to sell some of this property to settle his debts. (2,89 8/23/1786)

375. Mr. Webster will deliver his second lecture tomorrow at the Assembly Room. (2,89 8/23/1786)

376. Jeremiah Libbey has bohea tea and salt for sale. (2,89 8/23/1786)

377. Ship News:

		ENTERED FROM
Brig *Polly*	Rice	Martinico
		CLEARED FOR
Brig *Viscomdte D'Arrott*	Mendum	Tobago
Brig *Dispatch*	Tibbets	West Indies

(2,90 8/30/1786)

378. On September 21, a public vendue will be held on the premises, near Church Hill, to sell a two story home, with a barn, large garden, two good springs, a wharf, and water privileges. This home is part of the estate of widow Alice Hight, deceased and formerly the property of Charles Hight, deceased. For details apply to Nathaniel Shannon, Administrator of the estate. Portsmouth, September 6, 1786. (2,90 8/30/1786)

379. Ship News:

		CLEARED FOR
Schooner *Polly*	Briard	West Indies

(2,91 9/6/1786)

380. Billings Putnam announces that he conducts a blacksmith business at Capt. George Hart's shop. (2,91 9/6/1786)

381. Ship News:

		ENTERED FROM
Schooner *Polly*	Chase	Carolina
Sloop *Mary*	Fernald	Guadaloupe
Brig *Nancy*	Frost	Tobago
Brig *Astrea*	Salter	Cape Francois
		CLEARED FOR
Brig *Pomona*	Horney	Great Britain
Brig *Izette*	Sargent	West Indies
Sloop *Dolphin*	Coffin	St. Peters
Schooner *Success*	Fernald	West Indies

(2,92 9/13/1786)

382. J. Pearson, Sec'y, attests that a petition has been preferred to the General Court by Azariah Webb seeking the right to keep

a ferry on the Connecticut River between Capt. Richard Young's farm, in the southwest corner of Piermont and Capt. Uriah Stone's farm in Piermont.   Concord, June 10, 1786.   (2,92 9/13/1786)

383.   All persons with demands on the estate of Ebenezer Green, of Lyme, New Hampshire, deceased, represented insolvent, are requested to contact Davenport Phelps, Russel Freeman and Jonathan Franklin, Commissioners.   They will conduct business at the home of Mrs. Dorcas Green, in Lyme, on the third Tuesday of the next six months. Lyme, September 1, 1786. (2,92 9/13/1786)

384.   Archelaus Temple forbids any person from trusting his wife, Lucy, on his account as she has eloped from his house. Westmoreland, August 1, 1786. (2,92 9/13/1786)

385. Ship News:

		ENTERED FROM
Sloop *Three Friends*	McElcheran	St. Peters
		CLEARED FOR
Schooner *Sukey*	Downes	S. Carolina
Schooner *Tryall*	Chamberlain	West Indies
Brig *Dover*	Manning	West Indies

(2,93 9/20/1786)

386.   J. Parker, Sheriff, announces that the sale of masts, yards and bowsprits will be postponed until the third Tuesday in October. Portsmouth, September 19, 1786. (2,93 9/20/1786)

387.   James Gooch will open a private school for misses and gentlemen on October 1. He will teach reading, writing and arithmetic. (2,93 9/20/1786)

388. Ship News:

		ENTERED FROM
Brig *Mary*	Shores	Guadaloupe
Brig *Endeavor*	Riley	St. Bartholomew

(2,94 9/27/1786)

389. James Calef, excise master for Grafton, requests all taverners and retailers to settle their excise with him for October 1785 to October 1786 by October 20, at his shop at Dover Landing. (2,94 9/27/1786)

390. Ship News:

		ENTERED FROM
Sloop *Emelia*	Kinghorn	Halifax
		CLEARED FOR
Brig *Betsy*	Hall	West Indies
Brig *Three Brothers*	Sherbourne	West Indies

(2,95 10/4/1786)

391. Died: At Portsmouth, Mrs. Mary Donaldson, 47. (2,95 10/4/1786)

392. J. Sullivan, Capt. General, has placed Col. Benjamin Stone, of the 20th regiment; Maj. James Cochran, of the 11th regiment; Lt. Asa Robinson, of the 11th regiment; Capt. John McKeen and Lt. Thomas McClary, both of the 8th regiment; and Capt. Ela Dow, Lt. Clough and Ens. Thomas Cotton, of the 7th regiment under arrest for exciting the citizens of New Hampshire to overturn the constitution and government of the state. Their cases will be heard before a General Court Martial at Exeter on November 21, with Maj. General Cilley as President. Col. Amos Cogswell, Col. Moses Leavet, Col. James Hill, Col. John Calef, Col. Michael McClary, LCol. James Hacket, LCol. E. Giddinge, LCol. Jonathan Cram, LCol. W. Brewster, LCol. Joseph Marsh, Maj. Jonathan Cass, Capt. George Hart and Capt. Thomas Shannon are appointed members of the Court. Col. Jonathan Rawson is appointed judge advocate. Durham, September 27, 1786. (2,95 10/4/1786)

393. J. Sullivan, Capt. General, has announced the following review schedule: third regiment on October 9 at Hampton; 18th regiment on October 11 at Deerfield; 11th regiment on October 13 at Concord; 22nd regiment on October 17 at Boscawen; 14th regiment on October 19 at Col. Webster's in Plymouth; 13th regiment on October 24 at Haverhill; 1st, 4th and 5th companies of the 25th regiment on October 25 at Major Young's in

Gunthwait; 2nd, 3rd and 6th companies of the same regiment on October 27 at Capt. David Page's in Lancaster; 31st regiment on October 31 at Darthmouth College; 15th regiment on November 2 at Cornish; 16th regiment on November 7 at Alstead; 21st regiment on November 9 at Chesterfield; 6th regiment on October 10 at Swanzey and 12th regiment on November 14 at Jaffrey. Exeter, September 19, 1786. (2,95 10/4/1786)

394.   Ship News: On October 13, the brig *Pomona*, Gilbert Horney, en route Liverpool from Portsmouth put into Casco Bay suffering the effects of a gale. All masts and deck gear had been carried away. Five crew members had been washed over board and only two were recovered. Last Sunday the ship *Viscomdte de Arrot*, John Palmer, arrived in Portsmouth in 82 days from Harve de Grace. It has also encountered a gale in which it lost main and mizzen masts and suffered much damage. Also a young lad was washed over board. (2,97 10/18/1786)

395.   Ship News:

		ENTERED FROM
Sloop *Dolphin*	Coffin	St. Peters
Schooner *Union*	Salter	Demerara
Schooner *Polly*	Parkinson	Shelburne
Brig *Port-Roseway*	Wishart	Shelburne
		CLEARED FOR
Ship *Charlotte*	Mountford	G. Britain
Brig *Endeavor*	Riley	West Indies
Sloop *Three Brothers*	McElcheran	Tobago
Sloop *Emelia*	Kinghorn	Halifax

(2,97 10/18/1786)

396.   At a meeting of proprietors of Franconia will be held at the home of Amos Sawyer, innholder in Plaistow, on May 22, 1786.   There a tax rate was approved and Isaac Searle was selected Collector of this tax.   He advises that unless the taxes are paid to him at his home in Williamstown, MA, or to Amos Sawyer in Plaistow in eight weeks, their lands will be put up for sale. Plaistow, October 1,1786. (2,97 10/18/1786)

397. The collection of books known as the Social Library will be sold on October 31 at the Union Hall in Portsmouth. People holding books from the library are requested to return them to Rev. Joseph Buckingham, librarian. Samuel Penhallow, P. C., Portsmouth, October 9, 1786. (2,97 10/18/1786)

398. All persons with demands on the estate of Jeremiah Brient, late of Newmarket, deceased, are again requested to settle the same with Walter Brient, administrator. Newmarket, October 17, 1786. (2,97 10/18/1786)

399. Died: At Portsmouth, Benjamin Drown; a child of Robert Neal; a child of John Goodwin; Mrs. Abigail True, 67, wife of Israel True and; Mrs. Margery Clark, wife of Joseph Clark. (2,98 10/25/1786)

400. Ship News:

		ENTERED FROM
Ship *Viscomte d'Arrot*	Palmer	Havre
		CLEARED FOR
Schooner *Polly*	Parkinson	Shelburne
Sloop *Mary*	Palmer	South Carolina

(2,98 10/25/1786)

401. William Brewster has moved from his house on Congress Street where he operated a tavern to an elegant home on Court Street, which was previously occupied by President Langdon and which is commonly known as Packer's House. There he will operate a coffee house and tavern. Portsmouth, October 25, 1786. (2,98 10/25/1786)

402. Joshua Foss Jr. advises the proprietors of Barrington that he will be working on the state road in Barrington. Anyone interested in working with him should meet him at the home of Capt. Philip Caverly, in Barrington, on November 7. Barrington 23, 1786. (2,98 10/25/1786)

403. Robert Gerrish will sell, at his printing office on Congress Street, Portsmouth, a 1787 almanac by Daniel Sewell. (2,98 10/25/1786)

404. All persons who have demands on the estate of Gregory Purcell, late of Portsmouth, deceased, are requested to present them to Sarah Purcell, Executrix, for settlement. Portsmouth, October 23, 1786. (2,98 10/25/1786)

405. Ship News:

		ENTERED FROM
Sloop *Randolph*	Gardner	Trinadad
Schooner *Nancy*	Brown	Demerara

(2,99 11/1/1786)

406. The following people had letters at the post office in Portsmouth on October 31:

•A: John Atkins, Rochester; Ellis Amee, Kittery; Katty Andrews, Windham

•B: John Bevans, Wendell; Jonathan Blake, Kingston; Isaac Blaisdell, New Salisbury; Samuel Bragg, Dover; Moses Barnett, Londonderry; Robert Barlley, Londonderry; James Bettan, Windham; Tobias Butler, New Boston

•C: Jonathan Clark, Exeter; Mons. Capelle Cherugion, Hampton; Nat. Conant, Sanford; Joseph Clark, Durham; George Calder, Portsmouth; James Calef, (3), Dover; John Colcord, Newmarket; Thomas Cochran, Boston

•E: Rev. Nathaniel Ewer, Newmarket

•F: Gideon Frost, Uxbridge; Robert Fulton Sr, Londonderry; Zephaniah Fulton, Kingston; Robert S. French, Kingston

•G: Gen. Ichabod Goodwin, Berwick; Josiah Gilman, Exeter; John Gould, Portsmouth; Nabby Gay, Hinsdale; John Grant, Berwick; Abigail Hale, Kingston; Stephen Grover, Dartmouth; William Gale, Concord; William Grigg, Poplin

•H: John Henry Haines, Dover; Peter Hanyman, Plaistow; Samuel Harper, Ackworth; Samuel Huntly; Samuel Henry, Amherst; Sarah Hall, Durham Falla; Samuel Ham, Durham Falls; Joshua Hubbard, Kittery; Andrew Hill, Kittery; Jonathan Hamilton, Berwick; Jos. Hunt, Portsmouth

•J: Elijah Jenkins, Berwick; Noah Jackman, Plaistow; Daniel Jones, Hinsdale

•K: Rudolphus Kent, Concord

•L: Edward Low, York; Abigail Lowd, Portsmouth; William Lowd, Berwick

•M: Alexander McGooch, Berwick; Amos Moril, Epsom; William Meservey, Portsmouth; William Morris, Portsmouth; Luke Mills, Portsmouth

•N: John Nooman, Allentown

•O: William Odiorne, Newmarket; Israel Oat, Portsmouth; Anne Olisse, Portsmouth

•P: Stephen Parker, Durham; Thomas Patterson, Londonderry

•R: Jacob G. Russel, Guilford; Stephen Roberts, Dover; Nathaniel Rogers, Newmarket; Jeremiah Rodlin, New Castle; Samuel Robinson, Exeter; Bridget Ridgaway, Greenland; Ephraim Robinson, Exeter; Alexander Robinson, (2) Dearing

•S: Aaron Staniford, Portsmouth; Polly Stindon, Londonderry; Thomas Sparhawk, Walpole; Mary Sale, Portsmouth; William Stocker, New Castle; Robert Shearman, Exeter; Messers. Shaw & Calland, Kingston

•T: William Tredick, New Castle; Benjamin Tyler, Claremont; William Thornton, Thornton; Adonijah Tyler, Hopkinton; Daniel Tenney, Hopkinton

•W: Benjamin Woodbridge, New Castle; Asaph White, Charlemont; Timothy White, Dover; President Wheelock, Hanover; Jeremiah Wille, Durham

Note: Names are spelled as they appear on the letters.

(2,99 11/1/1786)

407.   Sarah Purcell has moved to the commodious house on Congress Street, previously occupied by Col. William Brewster. She has opened a tavern there. (2,99 11/1786)

408.   Died; At Portsmouth, two grand children of Daniel Simes, of Portsmouth. (2,100 11/8/1786)

409. Ship News:		ENTERED FROM
Schooner *Betsey*	Salter	St. Lucia
		CLEARED FOR
Sloop *Red Bird*	Currier	S. Carolina
(2,100 11/8/1786)		

410.   George Doig has a new fall back chaise for sale. (2,100 11/8/1786)

411. A hundred acre farm in Tamworth is for sale. For particulars contact Stephen Merrill at his home in Conway. (2,100 11/8/1786)

412. Ship News: ENTERED FROM
Ship *Hero*   Wardrobe   Tobago

                                              CLEARED FOR
Brig *Sophia*   Roberts   l'Orient
Ship *Atlantic*   Trefethen   West Indies
Sloop *Red Bird*   Currier   S. Carolina
(2,101 11/15/1786)

413. Died: At Portsmouth, a child of John Abbot of Portsmouth. (2,101 11/15/1786)

414. John Parker, V.M., announces that the hull of the brigantine *Pomona* and its cargo will be sold at public vendue on December 7 at Partridge's wharf. (2,101 11/15/1786)

415. Ship News: CLEARED FOR
Schooner *Union*   Tibbets   Demarara
Brig *Port Roseway*   Wishart   Shelburne
Brig *Caledonia*   Bucan   Halifax
(2,102 11/22/1786)

416. Ship News: ENTERED FROM
Schooner *Laborious*   Nicholas   St. Peters
Schooner *Polly*   Briard   Martinico
                                             CLEARED FOR
Brig *Susannah*   Parker   West Indies
Schooner *Polly*   White   West Indies
Schooner *Nancy*   Brown   Demerara
(2,103 11/29/1786)

417. By order of the court, J. Rawson, Judge Advocate, announces that the General Court Martial, with Maj. Gen. Cilley as President, will convene on December 1 at the Court House in Exeter. Exeter, November 22, 1786. (2,103 11/29/1786)

418. Ship News:

		ENTERED FROM
Schooner *Tryall*	Chamberlain	St. Eustatia
Brig *Cooper*	Sellers	West Indies
		CLEARED FOR
Ship *Viscomte D'Arrot*	Palmer	Tobago
		CLEARED FOR
Schooner *Mermaid*	Trefethren	Georgia
Brig *Polly*	Rice	West Indies
Brig *Olive*	Smallcorn	West Indies
Brig *John*	Yeaton	West Indies
Brig *Astrea*	Salter	Cape Francois

(2,104 12/6/1786)

419. The following is a list of civil, military and ecclesiastical departments in New Hampshire from June 1786 to June 1787:

PRESIDENT: John Sullivan

HONORABLE COUNCIL: Joshua Wentworth, Amos Shepard, Robert Means, Christopher Toppan, Moses Dow

SENATE:

Rockingham County

John McClary	Joseph Gilman
Joshua Wentworth	George Atkinson
John Bell	

Strafford County

| Otis Baker | John McDuffie |

Hillsborough County

| Matthew Thornton | Eben'r Webster |

Cheshire County

| John Bellows | Amos Shepard |

Grafton County

| Elisha Payne | Joseph Pearson, Sec'y |

John T. Gilman, Treasurer

Nathaniel Gilman, Loan Officer

Supply Clapp, Commissary General

Stephen Gorham, Commissioner of Continental Accounts for the state

John Langdon, Speaker

John Calfe, Clerk of the House

Justices of the Superior Court:

Samuel Livermore, Chief Justice Concord

Josiah Bartlett	Kingston
John Dudley	Raymond
Woodbury Langdon	Portsmouth

Benjamin West,
    Attorney General   Charlestown

Nathaniel Adams & Daniel Humphreys,
    Notaries Public   Portsmouth

Joshua Brackett,
    Judge, Maritime Court   Portsmouth

Justices of the Peace and for Quorum for the State:

Samuel Livermore	Concord
Josiah Bartlett	Kingston
John Dudley	Raymond
John Sullivan	Durham
Matthew Thornton	Merrimac
Nathaniel Folsom	Exeter
Ebenezer Thompson	Durham
Jonathan Blanchard	Dunstable
Samuel Ashley	Claremont
Benjamin Bellows	Walpole
John McClary	Epsom
Francis Blood	Temple
Joseph Badger	Gilmanton
Nathaniel Peabody	Atkinson
Moses Chase	Cornish
Woodbury Langdon	Portsmouth
George Atkinson	Portsmouth
Jonathan Moulton	Hampton
Moses Dow	Haverhill
John Sherburne	Portsmouth
Daniel Rindge	Portsmouth
John Langdon	Portsmouth

Civil Officers for Rockingham County

Justices of the Inferior Court of Common Pleas:

Nathaniel Folsom	Exeter
Timothy Walker	Concord
Abiel Foster	Canterbury

(Justices of the Inferior Court of Common Pleas)

John Calfe	Hampstead
John Parker, Sheriff	Portsmouth
Phillips White, Judge of Probate	South Hampton
William Parker, Registrar of Probate	

Justices of the Peace and of Quorum for Rockingham County:

Richard Downing	Newington
Samuel Penhallow	Portsmouth
Phillips White	South Hampton
Timothy Walker	Concord
John Langdon	Portsmouth
Samuel Emerson	Chester
Abiel Foster	Canterbury
Joseph Cilley	Nottingham
John Bell	Londonderry
Samuel Hale	Portsmouth
William Weeks	Greenland

Justices of the Peace for Rockingham County:

Samuel Little	Hampstead
Christopher Toppan	Hampton
William Knight	Portsmouth
Noah Emery	Exeter
William Parker	Exeter
Archelaus Moore	Canterbury
John Calfe	Hampstead
John Pickering	Portsmouth
Thomas Bartlett	Nottingham
Richard Bartlett	Pembroke
Joseph Gilman	Exeter
Mark Wiggin	Stratham
Enoch Coffin	Epping
Robert Wilson	Chester
James Gibson	Pelham
William Morrell	Brentwood
Samuel Weare	Hampton Falls
Josiah Adams	Newmarket
Michael McClary	Epsom

(Justices of the Peace for Rockingham County)

John Blunt	New Castle
Ephraim Pickering	Newington
Joseph Dow	Hampton
Winthrop Gove	Seabrook
Abraham Perkins	Epping
Peter Green	Concord
John Cram	Pittsfield
Nathan Batcheldor	Loudon
Josiah Gage	Pelham
John Bryant	Bow
Samuel Moores	Candia
Jeremiah Eastman	Deerfield
Jonathan Jenness	Northwood
George Gains	Portsmouth
Peter Clements	Atkinson
Clement Marsh	Greenland
Samuel Daniel	Pembroke
John Taylor Gilman	Exeter
George Reid	Londonderry
Josiah Gilman Jr.	Exeter
Joseph Pearson	Exeter
Archibald McMurphy	Londonderry
Jeremiah Fogg	Kensington
Joseph March	Deerfield
Josiah Flagg	Chester
Jabez Hoit	Chester
John Allen	Salem
Joseph Parsons	Rye
Samuel Gilman	Newmarket
John Neal	Londonderry
Jonathan Greeley Jr.	East Kingston
Ebenezer Clifford	Kensington
Matthias Bartlett	Newtown
Richard Jenness	Deerfield
Moody Morse	Salem
James Gilmore	Windham
Thomas Page	Hawke
Soloman Wheeler	Kingston

(Justices of the Peace for Rockingham County)

Moses Hook	Sandown
Jeremiah Clough Jr.	Canterbury
Thomas Gilman	Northfield
Nathaniel Batchelder	East Kingston
Levi Dearborn	North Hampton
Moses Leavitt	North Hampton
Benjamin Butler	Nottingham
Simon Wiggin	Stratham
Jonathan Leavitt	Chichester
Elisha Brown	Seabrook
Timothy Ladd	Salem
Eliphalet Poor	Hampstead
Samuel Jenness	Rye
Stephen March	Greenland
John Scribner	Poplin
John White	Plaistow
Oliver Whipple	Portsmouth
Jesse Johnson	Hampstead
Benjamin Sias	Loudon
James Betton	Windham
Nathaniel Dudley	Raymond
Joshua Weeks	Greenland
John Prentice	Londonderry
Joseph Demerit	Northwood
Jonathan Clark	Northwood
Joseph Welch	Plaistow
George Frost	New Castle

Coroners for Rockingham County:

Jeremiah Libbey	Portsmouth
Richard Champney	Portsmouth
Simon Wiggin	Stratham
Jonathan Garland	Hampton
Samuel Folsom	Exeter
Simon Jenness	Rye
Simonds Seacomb	Kingston
Henry Butler	Nottingham
James Gray	Epsom
Jonathan Eastman	Concord

(Coroners for Rockingham County)

Joseph Gregg	Londonderry
Moses Shaw	Kingston
Jacob Chase	Chester
John Dow Jr.	Atkinson
Daniel Page	Deerfield
Nehemiah Wheeler	Epping
Nathaniel Kimbell	Plaistow
William Duty	Salem
Eliphlet Poor	Hampstead
Robert Young	Pelham
Daniel McDuffee	
Jonathan Adams	
David Page	North Hampton
Peter Tilton	Hampton Falls
Caleb Sanborn	Hampton Falls
Stephen Chase	Chester
Benjamin Emerson	Hampstead
James Towle	Hawke
David George	Concord
James Aiken	Londonderry
Wentworth Chestwell	Newmarket
Samuel Chamberlain	Loudon
John Weeks	Greenland
John Morrison	Windham
Samuel McConnel	Pembroke
John Fabyan	Newington
Philip Towle	Hampton
Job Haskell	Pittsfield

Justices of the Inferior Court of Common Pleas for Strafford County:

George Frost	Durham
John Plummer	Dover
Thomas Cogswell	Gilmanton
Theophilus Dame, Sheriff	Dover

Joseph Badger, Judge of Probate

John Wentworth, Register of Probate

Justices of the Peace and Quorum for Strafford County:

George Frost	Durham

(Justices of the Peace and Quorum for Strafford County)

Otis Baker	Dover
John Plummer	Rochester
Moses Carr	Somersworth
Ebenezer Smith	Meredith
Simeon Dearborn	Wakefield

Justices of the Peace for Strafford County:

Henry Rust	Wolfeboro
Icabod Rollings	Somersworth
John Wentworth	Dover
Joseph Sias	Lee
Solomon Emerson	Madbury
Simeon Dearborn	Wakefield
Valentine Mathes	Durham
John Garland	Barrington
Daniel Bedee	Sandwich
Thomas Parsons	Effingham
James Knowles	Rochester
Hercules Mooney	Lee
David Page	Conway
David Gilman	Tamworth
Joseph Roberts	New Durham Gore
John Tasker	Barnstead
Thomas Cogswell	Gilmantown
Joshua Wingate	Dover
Joseph Badger Jr.	Gilmanton
Benning Moulton	New Hampton
Samuel Hale	Barrington
Thomas Tash	New Durham
John Leavitt	Effingham
Jacob Brown	Ossipee
Jabez Dame	Rochester
David Copp	Wakefield
John Smith 3rd	Durham
Daniel Sanborn	Sanbornton
William Harper	Sanbornton
Joshua Foss	Barrington
John Waldron	Dover
James Brackett	Lee

(Justices of the Peace for Strafford County)

Andrew McMillan	Conway
James Carr	Somersworth
John Rollins	Somersworth
Joseph Peirce	New Durham Gore
Avery Hall	Wakefield
Nathan Hoit	Moultonboro
Aaron Wingate	Rochester

Coroners of Strafford County:

Andrew Torr	Dover
Joseph Stevens	Durham
John Cate	Barrington
Jabez Dame	Rochester
Edward Gilman Jr.	Gilmantown
Nathaniel Shannon	Moultonboro
Timothy Meader	Tamworth
James Hearsey	Somersworth
John Gilman	Meredith
Thomas Chadbourne	Conway
Avery Hall	Wakefield
Eleazer Davis	New Durham Gore
James Brackett	Lee
Samuel Keille	Madbury
Josiah Main	Rochester

Justices of the Inferior Court of Common Pleas for Hillsborough County:

Timothy Farrar	New Ipswich
Francis Blood	Temple
James Underwood	Litchfield
Jeremiah Page	Dunbarton

Sheriff, Moses Kelley,

Judge of Probate, Jonathan Blanchard

Reg. of Probate, Samuel Dans

Justices of the Peace and of the Quorum for Hillsborough County:

Jonathan Lovewell	Dunstable
Matthew Patten	Bedford
James Underwood	Litchfield
John Hale	Hollis

(Justices of the Peace and of the Quorum for Hillsborough
County)

Timothy Farrar	New Ipswich
Jeremiah Page	Dunbarton
Moses Nichols	Amherst
John Stark	Derryfield

Justices of the Peace for Hillsborough County:

George Jackman	Boscawan
Isaac Andrews	Hillsboro
Robert MacGregore	Goffstown
Joseph Bartlett	Salisbury
Noah Worcester	Hollis
William South	Peterborough
John Robie	Weare
Joshua Bailey	Hopkinton
Benjamin Mann	Mason
John Cochran Jr.	New Boston
John Duncan	Antrim
Moses Little	Goffstown
Peter Clark	Lyndeboro
William Abbot	Wilton
Jonathan Weare	Andover
Ebenezer Rockwood	Wilton
John Preston	New Ipswich
Jonathan Searle	Mason
Henry Gerrish	Boscawen
Daniel Emerson Jr.	Hollis
Samuel Philbrick	Weare
Samuel Marsh	Nottingham West
Nathaniel Bean	Warner
Asa Davis	Nottingham West
Ebenezer Webster	Salisbury
John Hogg	Dunbarton
Matthew Pettingale	Salisbury
Zephaniah Clark	Fishersfield
Nenien Aiken	Dearing
Levi Spaulding	Lyndeboro
Matthew Wallace	Peterborough
Augustus Blanchard	Amherst

(Justices of the Peace for Hillsborough County)

Richard Cutts	Shannon Amherst
Enoch Sawyer	Goffstown
Samuel Douglas	Raby
Aaron Greeley	Hopkinton
John Shepard	Amherst
Samuel Wilkins	Amherst
Timothy Taylor	Merrimac
Robert Means	Amherst
Samuel Fowler	Boscawen
Timothy Gibson	Henniker
William McQueston	Litchfield
Benjamin Wadley	Sutton
James Hosley	Hancock
John Orr	Bedford
Simeon Cummings	Merrimac

Coroners for Hillsborough County:

Augustus Blanchard	Amherst
Jonathan Eastman	Hollis
Zaccheus Chandler	Bedford
Samuel Haywood	New Ipswich
John Hogg	Dunbarton
Ebenezer Webster	Salisbury
Joseph Simons	Hillsborough
Samuel Kimbell	Henniker
Elias Boynton	Temple
Samuel Moore	Peterborough
Jacob McGaw	Merrimac
Timothy Wortley	Weare
James Cardwell	New Boston
Jonathan Martin	Wilton
Abel Kimbell	Hopkinton
William Forsyth	Dearing
Daniel Campbell	Amherst
Robert Wilson	Peterborough
Daniel Gould	Lyndeboro
Samuel Douglas	Raby
Samuel Haywood	Amherst
Ebenezer Hunting	New London

(Coroners for Hillsborough County)
        John Dutton   Hillsboro
        (list to be continued in next issue) (2,105 12/13/1786)

420. Ship News: ENTERED FROM
Brig *Dover*   Manning   St. Bartholomew
Schooner *Success*   Furnell   Martinico
                                       CLEARED FOR
Brig *Abigail*   Peirce   West Indies
Sloop *Randolph*   Gardner   Trinidad
Schooner *Industry*   Peirce   West Indies
(2,105 12/13/1786)

421. Continuation of the list of civil, military and ecclesiastical
department for New Hampshire for June 1785 to June 1786:
Justices of the Inferior Court for Cheshire County
        Simeon Olcott   Charlestown
        Samuel Ashley   Claremont
        Benjamin Bellows   Walpole
        Francis Smith   Plainfield
        Samuel Hunt, Sheriff
        Thomas Sparhawk, Judge of Probate
        Michael Lawrence, Register of Probate
Justices of the peace and of the Quorum for Cheshire County:
        Samuel Chase   Cornish
        Simeon Olcott   Charlestown
        Enoch Hale   Rindge
        Benjamin West   Charlestown
Justices of the Peace for Cheshire County:
        Francis Smith   Plainfield
        Thomas Sparhawk   Walpole
        Joseph Greenwood   Dublin
        Thomas Baker   Keene
        Calvin Frink   Swanzey
        Moses Whipple   Craydon
        John Hubbard   Charlestown
        Charles Huntoon   Unity
        Abel Stevens   Grantham
        __salom Kingsbury   Alstead

(Justices of the Peace for Cheshire County)

Daniel Newcomb	Keene
Michael Cressey	Chesterfield
John Bellows	Walpole
Sanford Kingsbury	Claremont
Oliver Ashley	Claremont
___ Doolittle	Westmoreland
Samuel Holmes	Surry
William Ripley	Cornish
Samuel Kendell	Fitzwilliam
Samuel Griffin	Packersfield
___ Copland	Stoddard
Daniel Grout	Acworth
Daniel ___	Kimbell
Roger Gilman	Jaffrey
___ Stevens	Newport
Edward Jewett	Rindge
Jonathan Arnold	Winchester
Reuben Alexander	Winchester
Elijah Frink	Lempster
Amos Shepard	Alstead
Alexander Parkman	Marlborough
Elijah Grout	Charlestown
___ Young	Grantham
Samuel Works	Westmoreland
Joseph Roansevil	Washington
___ry Ingalls	

Coroners for Cheshire County:

George Kimbell	Charlestown
Isaac Hammond	Swanzey
James Philbrick	Rindge
Daniel Chase	Cornish
Samuel Trot	Walpole
Joseph Burt	Westmoreland
John Colburn	
___ Ames	Keene
Samuel Buss	
Isaac Temple	Alstead

Justices of the Inferior Court of Common Pleas for Grafton
     County:

Samuel Emerson	Plymouth
Bezal. Woodward	Hanover
James Woodward	Haverhill
Ezekiel Ladd	
David Webster, Sheriff	
Charles Johnston, Judge of Probate	
Moses Dow, Register of Probate	

Justices of the Peace and of the Quorum for Grafton County:

Samuel Emerson	Plymouth
Bezaliel Woodward	Hanover
Elisha Payne	Lebanon
Joseph Whipple	Dartmouth
Charles Johnston	Haverhill

Justices of the Peace for Grafton County:

Daniel Brainard	Rumney
Charles Johnston	Haverhill
Enoch Page	Wentworth
Francis Worcester	Plymouth
James Woodward	Haverhill
Edwards Bucknam	Lancaster
Jeremiah Eams	Northumberland
Joshua Copp	Warren
Thomas Russell	Piermont
Joshua Tolford	Alexandria
Carr Huse	New Castle
Davenport Phelps	Orford
Moses Baker	Campton
Jonathan Child	Lyme
William Ayer	Cannan
John Rogers	Plymouth
Jonathan Blake	Landaff
Eliha Hide	Lebanon
Jacob Hurd	Bath
Noah Worcester Jr.	Thornton
Jonathan Freeman	Hanover
Jesse Johnson Jr.	Enfield
Russell Freeman	Hanover

(Justices of the Peace for Grafton County)

Joseph Skinner	Grafton
Joseph Seater	Plymouth
Samuel Todd	Orford
Edmond Shattuck	Cockermouth
Ebenezer Green	Lyme
John Wheatley	Lebanon
Ebenezer Hoit	Grafton
Alexander Craige	Rumney
George W.	Livermore
Aaron Hutchinson	Lebanon

Coroners for Grafton County:

James Brown	Stratford
Joshua Harris	Canaan
Alexander Craige	Rumney
Russell Freeman	Hanover
Uriah Stone	Piermont
Joshua Young	Haverhill
Daniel Heath	New Chester
William George	Plymouth
Jesse Young	Guntwaite
James Sawyer	Landaff
James Gould	Hanover
Nathaniel Rogers	Orford
John Colburn Jr.	Lebanon
Abraham Burnham	Rumney
John Fairfield	Lyme
Samuel Worcester	Wentworth

(to be continued in next issue) (2,106 12/20/1786)

422.   Died: At Portsmouth, John Rindge, 60; Mrs. Olive Rindge, comfort of Daniel Rindge and daughter of Maj. William Gardner, of Portsmouth. (2,106 12/20/1786)

423. Ship News:		ENTERED FROM
Brig *Visc'te d'Arrot*	Mendum	Martinico
Brig *Dispatch*	Wingate	St. Bartholomew
		CLEARED FOR
Sloop *Mary*	Gunnison	Tobago

Ship *Elizabeth*   Seaward   Bristol
(2,106 12/20/1786)

424.   There is a fine working yoke of oxen for sale at Gerrish's printing office, Congress Street, Portsmouth. (2,106 12/20/1786)

425.   List of civil, military and ecclesiastical departments of New Hampshire from June 1786 to June 1787 continued: Generals and Field Officers:

    John Sullivan, Capt. General
    Benjamin Bellows, 1st Maj. General
    Joseph Cilley, 2nd Maj. General

Brigadier Generals with the uniforms of their brigades:

	Colors	Facing
Johatnan Moulton	white	deep crimson
George Reid	white	deep blue
Moses Dow	white	bright scarlet
Jonathan Blanchard	white	green
Jonathan Chase	white	sky blue
Thomas Bartlett	white	black

Field Officers of the Train Band
    1st regiment

Peirce Long, Col.	Portsmouth
Mark Wiggins, LCol.	Stratham
_____, Maj.	
Joseph Parsons, 2nd Maj.	Rye

    2nd regiment

Theophilus Dame, Col.	Dover
Jona. Wentworth, LCol.	Somersworth
David Place, Maj.	Rochester
Samuel Hale, 2nd Maj.	Barrington

    3rd regiment

Moses Leavitt, Col.	N. Hampton
Jonathan Cram, LCol.	Hampton Falls
Joseph Clifford, Maj.	Kensington
Josiah Dearborn, 2nd Maj.	Hampton

    4th regiment

James Hill, Col.	Newmarket
Eliphalet Giddinge, LCol.	Exeter

(Field Officers of the Train Band)

Porter Kimbell, Maj.	Brentwood
Benajmin Brown, 2nd Maj.	Epping

5th regiment

Noah Lovewell, Col.	Dunstable
Samuel Chase, LCol.	Litchfield
James Ford, Maj.	
John Goss, 2nd Maj.	

6th regiment

Reuben Alexander, Col.	Winchester
Oliver Capron, LCol.	Richmond
Jonathan P. Whitcomb, Maj.	
Daniel Ashley, 2nd Maj.	Winchester

7th regiment

John Calfe, Col.	Kingston
David Quimby, LCol.	Hawke
Philip Tilton, Maj.	East Kingston
Joseph Tilton, 2nd Maj.	

8th regiment

Daniel Reynolds, Col.	Londonderry
James Gilman, LCol.	Windham
Joseph Gregg, Maj.	Londonderry
Thomas Hardy, 2nd Maj.	

9th Regiment

10th regiment

Ebenezer Smith, Col.	Meredith
Joseph Badger Jr., LCol.	Gilmanton
Chase Taylor, Maj.	Sanbornton
Richard Sinkler, 2nd Maj.	Barnstead

11th regiment

Aaron Kinsman, Col.	Concord
Jeremiah Clough Jr., LCol.	Canterbury
James Cochran, Maj.	Pembroke
Joseph Tilton, 2nd Maj.	Loudon

12th regiment

Francis Blood, Col.	Temple
Philip Putnam, LCol.	Wilton
Ezra Town, Maj.	
Samuel Gregg, 2nd Maj.	

(Field Officers of the Train Band)
 13th regiment

Azariah Webb, Col.	Piermont
Obediah Clement, LCol.	Warren
Uriah Stone, Maj.	Piermont
Joshua Young, 2nd Maj.	Haverhill

 14th regiment

Moses Baker, Col.	Campton
Alexander Craige, LCol.	Rumney
Benjamin Gould, Maj.	
M. Dwyer, 2nd Maj.	New Holderness

 15th regiment

Samuel Ashley Jr., Col.	Claremont
Moses Whipple, LCol.	Craydon
Joseph Kimbell, Maj.	Plainfield
Diah Spaulding, 2nd Maj.	

(to be continued in the next issue) (2,107 12/27/1786)

426. Ship News:

		ENTERED FROM
Brig *Kitty*	Thwing	Tobago
Brig *Izette*	Sergant	St. Eustatia
Ship *Amazon*	Floyd	Halifax
		CLEARED FOR
Schooner *Blossom*	Trandy	Demerara

(2,107 12/27/1786)

427. Lamson and Ranlet of Exeter will soon publish an address concerning the present political situation in America. (2,107 12/27/1786)

428. The following is a continuation of the lists of civil, military and ecclesiastical department of New Hampshire from June 1786 to June 1787:

(Field Officers of the Train Band)
 16th regiment

Amos Shepard, Col.	Alstead
Josiah Goldsmith, LCol.	Walpole
Silas Wright, Maj.	Stoddard
Timothy Fletcher, 2nd Maj.	

(Field Officers of the Train Band)

17th regiment

Nathaniel Emerson, Col.	Candia
William White, LCol.	Chester
Stephen Dearborn, Maj.	
Daniel Norris, 2nd Maj.	Raymond

18th regiment

Michael McClary, Col.	Epsom
Joseph March, LCol.	Deerfield
Joseph Harvey, Maj.	Northwood
Henry Butler, 2nd Maj.	Nottingham

19th regiment

John Palmer, Col.	Wakefield
Nathan Hoit Jr., LCol.	Moultonboro
Jacob Smith, Maj.	Sandwich
Joshua Heath, 2nd Maj.	Conway

20th regiment

Benjamin Stone, Col.	Atkinson
Abraham Dow, LCol.	
Ezekiel Gile, Maj.	
Moses Little, 2nd Maj.	

21st regiment

G. Aldrich, Col.	Westmoreland
Joseph Burt, LCol.	
Jonathan Smith, Maj.	Surrey
Ebenezer Britton, 2nd Maj.	

22nd regiment

Eben. Webster, Col.	Salisbury
Joshua Bayley, LCol.	
Robert Wallace, Maj.	
Enoch Gerrish, 2nd Maj.	

23rd regiment

Daniel Rand, Col.	
Jedediah Sanger, LCol.	Jaffrey
Sylvanus Reed, Maj.	
Richard Roberts, 2nd Maj.	

24th regiment

Ebenezer Brewster, Col.	Hanover
Edmund Freeman, LCol.	Lebanon

(Field Officers of the Train Band)
    Samuel Jones, Maj.
    _____, 2nd Maj.
  25th regiment

J. Whipple, Col.	Dartmouth
Edwards Bucknam, LCol.	Lancaster
John Young, Maj.	Gunthwaite
Asa Bayley, 2nd Maj.	Landass

Field Officers of the Artillery

Thomas Thompson, Col.	Portsmouth
James Hackett, LCol.	Exeter
Caleb Hogdon, 2nd LCol.	Dover
Samuel Akinson, Maj.	Boscawen
Samuel Young, 2nd Maj.	

General and Field Officers of the Light Horse
Nathaniel Peabody, Brigadier General
1st regiment

Amos Cogswell, Col.	Dover
William Brewster, LCol.	Portsmouth
Jonathan Cass, Maj.	Exeter

2nd regiment

_____, Col.	
Peter Green, LCol.	Concord
Davenport Phelps. Maj.	Orford

3rd regiment
    _____, Col.
    _____, LCol.
    _____, Maj.

(to be continued) (3,108 1/3/1787)

429. Married: At Portsmouth last Sunday by Rev. Mr. Buckminster, James Sullivan, of Boston, to Mrs. Martha Simpson, of Portsmouth, relict of the late Thomas Simpson, commander of the continental frigate *Ranger*; and yesterday by Rev. Mr. Buckminster, Charles Treadwell, 82, to Mrs. Phebe Dennet, 67, both of Portsmouth. (3,108 1/3/1787)

430. Ship News:

		CLEARED FOR
Brig *Irish Gamblet*	Turner	West Indies

Ship *Exeter*	McClure	West Indies
Brig *Montpelier*	Miller	West Indies
Ship *Hero*	Wardrobe	West Indies
(3,108 1/3/1787)		

431. Samuel Hill has for sale blankets and other merchandise just imported from London. (3,108 1/3/1787)

432. Died: At Portsmouth, Mark Nelson, goldsmith, after a long illness. (3,109 1/10/1787)

433. Ship News:

		ENTERED FROM
Schooner *Rosannah*	Lovett	N. Brunswick
		CLEARED FOR
Schooner *Polly*	Briard	West Indies
Brig *Nancy*	Frost	West Indies
Schooner *Tryall*	Chamberlain	West Indies
Brig *Two Sisters*	Roach	West Indies
(3,109 1/10/1787)		

434. A house, located between the South School and Capt. William Furnald's, with a good barn, garden and well, is for let. For particulars contact John Gardner Jr. Portsmouth, Jan. 10, 1787. (3,109 1/10/1787)

435. Major Jonathan Cass has been appointed to command the Federal troops now being raised in New Hampshire. Samuel Cherry, William Morris, Josiah Monroe and Daniel Gookla have also been appointed to serve as captains in this corps. (3,109 1/10/1787)

436. Ship News:

		ENTERED FROM
Brig *Three Brothers*	Sherburne	St. Eustatia
CLEARED FOR		
Sloop *Endeavor*	York	West Indies
Schooner *Rosannah*	Lovett	N. Brunswick
(3,110 1/17/1787)		

437. The following is a continuation of the New Hampshire Register:

Trustees of the Phillips Exeter Academy:

John Phillips	Daniel Tilton
Thomas Odiorne	Rev. Benjamin Thurston
John Pickering	Rev. David McClure
Samuel Phillips	

Attorneys practicing at the Superior Court:

Benjamin Wentworth, Attorney General	Charlestown
William Parker	Exeter
John Pickering	Portsmouth
Joshua Atherton	Amherst
Oliver Whipple	Portsmouth
John Prentice	Londonderry
Peter Green	Concord
John Wentworth	Dover
Richard Cutts	
Shannon Hollis	
Moses Dow	Haverhill
Daniel Humphreys	Portsmouth
Jonathan M. Seawall	Portsmouth
Daniel Newcomb	Keene
Aaron Hutchinson	Lebanon
Oliver Peabody	Exeter
Samuel Dana	Amherst
Asa Dunbar	Keene
Edward S. Livermore	Concord
John Porter	Plymouth
Ebenezer Smith	Durham
Jonathan Rawson	Dover
Samuel Sherburne Jr.	Portsmouth

Attorneys practicing at the Inferior Court:

Noah Cook	New Ipswich
Clifton Clagett	Litchfield
Jeremiah Smith	Peterborough
William King	Dover
Alpheus Moore	Keene
Henry Mellen	Dover

(Attorneys practicing at the Inferior Court)
    George Pierce   Portsmouth
List of ministers, churches and religious assemblies:
    Rev. Joseph Buckminister   Portsmouth
    Samuel Haven, D.D.   Portsmouth
    John C. Ogden, Epis.   Portsmouth
    Noah Parker, Universalist   Portsmouth
    John Sparhawk and Daniel Humphreys,
        Sandemanians   Portsmouth
    Rev. Samuel McClintock   Greenland
    Huntington Porter   Rye
    Benjamin Thurston   Northampton
    Ebenezer Thayer   Hampton
    Samuel Langdon, D.D.   Hampton Falls
    Vacant Friends   Seabrook
    Oliver Noble   New Castle
    Isaac Mansfield   Exeter
    J. Miltemore and S. Shepard   Stratham
    Vacant N. Ewers   Newmarket
    Jeremiah Fogg   Kensington
    Vacant   Newington
    William Davison   Londonderry
    J. Morrison
    Ebenezer Flagg   Chester
    Nathaniel Noyes   Southampton
    Vacant   East Kingston
    Elihu Thayer   Kingston
    Josiah Stearns   Epping
    Vacant   Nottingham
    Timothy Upham & Eli Smith   Deerfield
    Vacant   Canterbury
    Jonathan Eames   Newton
    Vacant   Northwood
(list to be continued) (3,110 1/17/1787)

438. The General Court concluded its session in Portsmouth
last Thursday. Included in the acts passed was one granting
Benjamin Dearborn, of Portsmouth, the exclusive right of
making and vending engines and scales for the next fourteen

years. The General Court will convene June 6 in Concord. (3,111 1/24/1787)

439. The following is a continuation of the New Hampshire Register:
List of ministers, churches and religious assemblies:

Zac. Colby	Pembroke
Joseph Prince	Candia
Vacant	Hawke
Samuel Collins	Sandown
Stephen Peabody	Atkinson
Giles Merrill	Plaistow
Abner Bailey	Salem
Sim. Williams	Windham
Vacant	Pelham
Nathaniel Trask	Brentwood
Vacant	Concord
_____ Hazletine	Epsom
Vacant	Hampstead
Vacant	Raymond
Benjamin Balch	Barrington
Nathaniel Porter	Conway
Vacant	Dover
Friends	Dover
Curtis Coe	Durham
Isaac Smith	Gilmanton
Vacant	Lee
William Hooper	Madbury
Vacant	Middletown
Nicholas Folsom	Meredith
Jeremiah Shaw	Moultonboro
Vacant	New Durham
Joseph Haven	Rochester
Joseph Woodman	Sanbornton
James Pike	Somersworth
Asa Piper	Wakefield
Jeremiah Barnar &	
_____ Bruce	Amherst
Vacant	Bedford

(List of ministers, churches and religious assemblies)

Samuel Wood	Boscawen
Joseph Kidder	Dunstable
Cornelius Waters	Goffstown
Vacant	Henniker
Vacant	Litchfield
Jonathan Barns	Hillsborough
Daniel Emerson	Hollis
Vacant	Hopkinton
Sewall Goodridge	Lyndeboro
Vacant	Mason
Jacob Burnap	Merrimac
Soloman Moore	New Boston
Stephen Farrer	New Ipswich
Nathaniel Merrill	Nottingham West
David Annin	Peterborough
Samuel Ambrose	Sutton
Jonathan Searle	Salisbury
Manore Miles	Temple
Friends	Weare
William Kelly	Warner
Abel Fisk	Wilton
Jacob Mann	Alstead
Buckley Olcot	Charleston
Vacant	Cornish
Abraham Wood	Chesterfield
Edward Sprague	Dublin
Stephen Brigham	Fitzwilliam
Bunker Gay	Hinsdale
Lab. Ainsworth	Jaffrey
Aaron Hall	Keene
Eleazer Beckwith	Marlow
Vacant	Marlborough
John Ramele	Newport
Ab. Carpenter	Plainfield
Jacob Foster	Packersfield
Seth Payson	Rindge
Dury Bellows	Richmond
Edward Goddard	Swanzey

(List of ministers, churches and religious assemblies)

Vacant	Surry
Thomas Fessenden	Walpole
Vacant	Westmoreland
Vacant	Winchester
George Leslie	Wahington
Seldon Church	Campton
Thomas Baldwin	Canaan
Sylvanus Ripley,	
John Smith, &	
Eden Burroughs	Hanover
Isaiah Potter	Lebanon
William Conant	Lyme
Vacant	Orford
Nathan Ward	Plymouth
John Richards	Piermont
Vacant	Rumney
Vacant, Epis.	Haverhill
Experience Easterbrook	Thornton

(3,111 1/24/1787)

440. Ship News:

		ENTERED FROM
Sloop *Catharine*	Gerrish	St. Bartholomew
Brig *Dauphin*	Cutts	Port-au-Prince
Brig *Mary*	Stokell	Poole

(3,111 1/24/1787)

441. Ship News:

		CLEARED FOR
Schooner *Betsey*	Salter	West Indies
Sloop *Sally*	Smith	West Indies
Brig *Carbonear*	Briard	West Indies
Brig *Mary Ann*	Gerrish	West Indies

(3,112 1/31/1787)

442. Jonathan Moulton, of Hampton, has four farms for sale or long term lease. One farm is in Tamworth and is known as the Great Vineyard Farm. It consists of 2400 acres. The second is the Post Farm in Orford. It contains 690 acres and it lies on both sides of the great road leading from Charlestown, by Dartmouth

College, to Haverhill. The third property is the Governour's Farm in Piermont. This farm has about 600 acres. The fourth farm is the Great Interval Farm in Tamworth containing 2400 acres. He also has a selection of lots in Orford, Piermont, Haverhill, Lyman, Gunthwait, Wentworth, Warren, Moultonboro, New Hampton, Tamworth Burton, Eaton, and Chatham. (3,112 1/31/1787)

443. Thomas Young has a $50 note in hand signed by Job Savage in 1784. This note was given to Edward Smith of Newmarket and has been paid. (3,112 1/31/1787)

444. John Sullivan, Capt. General, issues a General Order concerning the General Court Martial held at Exeter with Major General Cilley presiding. He approves the punishment to Capt. James Cochran, Lt. Asa Robinson, Capt. John McKeen, Capt. Ela Dow, Lt. Clough and Ensign Thomas Cotton of being cashiered. He does not approve of the part of the punishment that called for future disqualification. Col. Benjamin Stone has been aquitted by the court martial and returned to duty. Major James Cochran was sentenced to be cashiered and then to be restored. This sentence is agreed with in that he has had an exemplary life except for this small error. Lt. Weare is awarded the same punishment. Lt Thomas McClary, being providentially prevented from attending the court martial is restored to duty. Quartermaster Brown was sentenced to a reprimand. This sentence is disapproved and he is restored to duty. Durham, January 29, 1787. (3,113 2/7/1787)

445. Ship News:

		CLEARED FOR
Snow *Nine Sons*	Stacy	West Indies
Brig *Mary*	Shores	West Indies
Ship *Amazon*	Floyd	West Indies

(3,113 2/7/1787)

446. Samuel Bean continues to ride post between Portsmouth and Amherst. Anyone with requests for Bean should leave them at one of the following houses of entertainment: Libbey, Greenland; Chase, Stratham; Folsom, Exeter; Tole, Hawk; Bell,

Chester; Martin and Jones, Londonderry; McQuiston, Litchfield; Taylor, Merrimac; Smith and Woodbury, Amherst; McLaughlin, New Boston; Fifield, Hale's Town; Wiggin, Hopkington; Kinsman, Concord; and Bartlett, Pembrook. (3,113 2/7/1787)

447. Died: At Portsmouth, John Lang, 65; a child of Dr. Nathanial Haven; and a child of John Reed. At Boston, Rev. Charles Chauncy, pastor of the First Church of Christ in Boston. (3,114 2/14/1787)

448. Ship News:

		ENTERED FROM
Ship *Cato*	Stevens	St. Ubes
		CLEARED FOR
Brig *Dover*	Manning	West Indies
Schooner *Success*	Jackson	West Indies

(3,114 2/14/1787)

449. Wall pew #4 in Mr. Parker's meeting house will be sold cheap for cash. (3,114 2/14/1787)

450. Ship News: On February 11, a 90 ton sloop en route Newbury from Sheepscot was washed ashore on the south side of Bang's Island near the mouth of Portland Harbor. The captain, Moses Chace, and a lad, John Deane, drowned. Their bodies were taken to Portland for burial. Three other crew members made it to shore on pieces of wreckage. They were taken in by the McIntosh family. (3,115 2/21/1787)

451. On February 11 in Hampton, the stable of General Moulton located near his home was consumed by fire. The fire was started by a boy carelessly handling a candle. (3,115 2/21/1787)

452. Died: At Portsmouth, Mrs. Mary Gray, 65; and a child of Mark Lang, both of Portsmouth. At Wakefield on February 5, Robert Macklin, 115, baker, formerly of Portsmouth, after seven or eight days illness. His eye sight and faculties remained good until a short time before his death. Macklin, at age 80,

frequently walked to Boston on foot returning the next day. (3,115 2/21/1787)

453. Ship News: CLEARED FOR
Brig *Viscomte D'Arrot*   Mendum   West Indies
(3,115 2/21/1787)

454. Daniel Symes has a new assortment of goods for sale at his shop on Congress Street, Portsmouth. (3,115 2/21/1787)

455. Jonathan Moulton, Brigadier General, orders the men of Portsmouth on the Alarm List to muster at the State House in Portsmouth on February 26. This meeting is to determine the alarm companies of Portsmouth and select officers. The Alarm List consists of all persons under sixty years of age, who do not belong to the Training Band, or otherwise excused by law. (3,115 2/21/1787)

456. Joseph Bass has for sale at his shop in Portsmouth, clover, herds grass and red top. (3,115 2/21/1787)

457. Betty Hickey, of Portsmouth, has the following tracts of land for sale: one whole right, #56, in Halifax, VT; 500 acres in the southwest part of Lempster, including a new barn; two whole rights in Bretton Woods. (3,115 2/21/1787)

458. At last Monday's meeting of the Alarm List, the following officers were selected:
        Col. George Gains
        LCol. Samuel Ham
        Maj. Jeremiah Libbey
Several men present agreed to form a company of foot. They selected the following officers:
        Capt. Elisha Hill
        Lt. Jeremiah Hill
        Ens. Mark Seavy (3,116 2/28/1787)

459. Ship News: ENTERED FROM
Schooner *Union*   Damrell   New York

CLEARED FOR
Brig *Cooper*   Sellars   West Indies
(3,116 2/28/1787)

460. Stephen Bartlett, constable advises the following non-residents have outstanding taxes for 1784 on lots in Pembroke. Unless paid, these lots will be sold at public vendue on March 19, at the home of Richard Bartlett of Pembroke:

Jonathan Rollings	Thomas Piper
Nathan Taylor	Benjamin Taylor
James Robinson	John Wentworth
Henry Wiggin	Benjamin Mason
William Burley	Daniel Moody
Walter Bryant	

(3,116 2/28/1787)

461. Capt. General John Sullivan announces that the uniform for the 2nd regiment of light horse under the command of Col. Green will be white waistcoat and breeches, and green coat faced with white. Portsmouth, February 28, 1787. (3,116 2/28/1787)

462. Josiah Bartlett, John McDuffie and Archibald McMurphy were chosen by the last session of the General Court to ascertain and fix the western line of a tract of land originally granted to Capt. John Mason. This line is known as the Masonian Line. The committee will hold a meeting at the home of Col. Eliphalet Giddinge at Exeter, on April 3. This meeting is open to the public. February 21, 1787. (3,116 2/28/1787)

463. Mrs. Homans proposes to open a school on the first Monday of April in her home which is opposite Dr. Hall Jackson's on Pitt Street. There she will teach needle work, reading, etc. Boarding of children will be provided for those who live a distance from the school. (3,117 3/7/1787)

464. Mary Nelson, Executrix, asks all persons who have demands on or who are indebted to the estate of Mark Nelson, late of Portsmouth, goldsmith, deceased, to present same for

prompt settlement. Portsmouth, March 6, 1787. (3,117 3/7/1787)

465. John Sullivan, Capt. General, presents a general order noting the schedule of inspections of troops throughout the state. The inspections start on April 23 and extend to May 31. He notes that Col. Cogswell will appear with as many of his companies of light horse as possible. Col. Michael Wentworth will do the same with his independent corps of horse. Durham March 7, 1787. (3,118 3/14/1787)

466. Voting has taken place in several towns. The following results are listed in descending order of votes received:
Portsmouth:
    For President: John Langdon, Samuel Livermore, President Sullivan.
    For Senators: Joshua Wentworth, John Langdon, John Bell, Peter Green, George Atkinson, Nathaniel Peabody, James Gibson, Archibald McMurphy, Joseph Gilman, John McClary.
Peter Green will represent Concord in the General Court.
Hopkington:
    For President: John Langdon, unanimous
Bascawen:
    For President: John Langdon, unanimous
Loudon:
    For President: President Sullivan, a majority
Londonderry:
    For President: President Sullivan, a majority
North Hampton:
    For President: Judge Livermore, unanimous
(3,118 3/14/1787)

467. Died: At Portsmouth, John Melcher, 78; and Mrs. Margaret Clemenson, 50, both of Portsmouth. (3,118 3/14/1787)

468. Ship News:

		ENTERED FROM
Sloop *Sylvenah*	Peamart	New Brunswick
Schooner *Rosannah*	Lovett	New Brunswick
Schooner *Adventure*	Trefethen	Baltimore

		CLEARED FOR
Brig *Dispatch*	Wingate	West Indies
Sloop *Sylvenah*	Peamart	New Brunswick
(3,118 3/14/1787)		

469. Ship News:		ENTERED FROM
Sloop *Henriette*	Whitney	Maryland
Brig *Olive*	Smallcorn	Tobago
		CLEARED FOR
Schooner *Rosannah*	Lovett	New Brunswick
(3,119 3/21/1787)		

470. John Gardner Jr. has a house with barn, garden and well for lease. It is located between the South School House and Capt. William Furnald's. (3,119 3/21/1787)

471. Samuel Hill has an assortment of recently imported goods for sale at his store opposite the market. (3,119 3/21/1787)

472. George Doig has a new elegant fall back chaise for sale along with other goods. (3,119 3/21/1787)

473. Lamson & Ranlet of Exeter have published an address to the public containing comments about the present political situation in America. It can be bought at the office of the publisher of this newspaper. (3,119 3/21/1787)

474. Ship News: Capt. William Vennard, who arrived in Portsmouth on March 19, advises the owners of the brigantine *Joseph*, Capt. Davis, arrived at James River, Virginia from Martinico on March 8. (3,120 3/28/1787)

475. Last Monday the inhabitants of Portsmouth met to vote for state offices. Daniel Rindge was selected moderator of the meeting. Results of voting listed in descending order are for President, John Langdon and President Sullivan and for senators George Atkinson, Joshua Wentworth, Samuel Hale, Thomas Odiorne, Christopher Toppan, John Sherburne, Peter Green, John Langdon, Jonathan Moulton, Jonathan Warner,

John McClary, James Hill and John Bell. John Pickering, John Sparhawk and George Gains were elected representatives. (3,120 3/28/1787)

476. Some voting returns from around the state were as follows: Unanimous for President Sullivan were Gilmanton, Brentwood, Dover and Northwood. Unanimous for Col. Langdon were Goffstown, Bedford, Richmond, Packerfield and Hollis. Divided between President Sullivan and Col. Langdon were Stratham and Newmarket. Divided between President Sullivan, Col. Langdon and Judge Livermore were Swanzey, and Kensington. (3,120 3/28/1790)

477. Ship News:		ENTERED FROM
Brig *Irish Gimblet*	Turner	Martinico
Sloop *Endeavour*	York	St. Bartholomew
		CLEARED FOR
Brig *Dauphin*	Cutts	West Indies

(3,120 3/28/1787)

478. William Dearing, Clerk, announces that Oliver Whipple, Commandant, has ordered the men of the Alarm List of the Southern District of Portsmouth to be ready for review on April 23. The Alarm List includes all men between forty and sixty. The Corps will meet at Rev. Mr. Haven's Meeting House in Portsmouth on April 16 to select Non-Commissioned Officers. Portsmouth, March 26, 1787. (3,120 3/28/1787)

479. All persons with demands on the estate of Lawrence Dowling, school master, late of Stratham, deceased, are to present them to Edward Dimsey, Administrator, for settlement. Portsmouth, March 27, 1787. (3,120 3/28/1787)

480. Nath'l Shannon has a house and lot in Portsmouth for sale. It is located by the ferry and was once a noted tavern. Portsmouth, March 27, 1787. (3,120 3/28/1787)

481. Samuel Bean announces that he will continue to ride post as he is at present. (3,120 3/28/1787)

482. At the annual Town Meeting, held on March 26, the following town officers were chosen:

Town Clerk—John Evans

Selectmen—George Gains, John Noble, Samuel Bowles and Nathaniel Treadwell

Assessors—Woodbury Langdon, Dr. A. R. Cutter, Col. Samuel Sherburne, Jeremiah Libbey and Samuel Sherburne (Plains)

Observers of the Poor—John Langdon, John Pickering, Dr. A. R. Cutter, Richard Champney, Jacob Sheafe Jr., Thomas Sheafe, Benjamin Dearborn, Moses Woodbury and Nathaniel Adams.

Auditors—John Sherburne, John Parker and Woodbury Langdon.

Agents—Samuel Penhallow and Samuel Cutts

Attorneys—John Pickering and Oliver Whipple

Firewards—Woodbury Langdon, John Parker, Joshua Wentworth, Ephraim Ham, John Noble, Jacob Treadwell, Jacob Sheafe Jr., William Gardner, Nathaniel Folsom, Jeremiah Libbey, James Sheafe and Aaron Hill

Constables—Clement March, ___ Chadburne, Edward Hart, Nahum Akerman, W. Vaughan and John Davenport

Lot Layers—Samuel Hale, W. Hart and Nathaniel Adams

Fence Viewers—Samuel Sherburne (Plains), Joseph Tucker, Capt. Samuel Hall, Abraham Elliott, W. Ham and Walter Akerman

Searchers and Sealers of Leather—G. Dame, Nathaniel Jackson and Perkins Ayers

Sealers of Weights and Measures—Daniel Lunt

Keeper of the Magazines—Jeremiah Libbey

Cullers and Packers of Fish—Joseph Walton, George Howe, George Hart and John Pitman

Pound Keeper—John Dennett

Measurers of Wood by Land and Water—John Beck, William Yeaton, Shackford Seaward, Samuel Beck, Ephraim Dennett, Henry Sherburne, Moses Melcher and William Moses

Corders of Wood—Joseph Benson, William Walden, Thomas Priest, Richard Peverly, Samuel Jones and George Walden

Hog Reeves—William Walden, Charles Waters, Sam'l Ham and Joseph Wincoll

School Committee — Rev. Dr. Haven, Rev. Joseph Buckminster, Rev. John C. Ogden, Samuel Hale, John Pickering and Dr. A. R. Cutter
Tything Men — Capt. Hall, Richard Jackson, Robert Ham, Joseph White, James Haslett and Samuel Moses. (3,121 4/4/1787)

483. Robert Gerrish has published and has for sale the Act for Forming and Regulating a Militia in New Hampshire. (3,121 4/4/1787)

484. T. Bartlet and John Cilley, Collectors of Excise, advise all persons in Rockingham County that those who have sold excisable liquors since October 1 that accounts must be settled by April 20 as per the law. Nottingham, April 2, 1787. (3,121 4/4/1787)

485. Died: At Portsmouth, Mrs. Martha Smith, 60; Mrs. Mary Ball, 62; and Mrs. Christian Place, 30, comfort of Samuel Place of Portsmouth. (3,122 4/11/1787)

486. Ship News:

		ENTERED FROM
Schooner *Industry*	Pierce	Philadelphia
Brig *Two Sisters*	Roach	Martinico
Schooner *Tryall*	Chamberlain	Baltimore
Brig *Nabby*	Kenney	Demerara

(3,122 4/11/1787)

487. Nathaniel Peabody, General of the Horse, orders all men in the Corps of Light Horse to be prepared for review as per the schedule published in the orders of the Capt. General of March 7. Atkinson, March 21, 1787. (3,122 4/11/1787)

488. Thomas Thompson will sail for London on April 25, 1787 in the brig *Kitty*. A prompt return is scheduled. Anyone desiring freight, should contact Thompson. Portsmouth, April 9, 1787. (3,122 4/11/1787)

489. Edmund H. Quincy has dirt free flax seed for sowing for sale at his store opposite the post office in Portsmouth. (3,122 4/18/1787)

490. The members of the New Hampshire Society of Cincinnati will meet at the home of Col. Samuel Folsom, in Exeter, on April 16, 1787. Durham, April 5, 1787. (3,122 4/18/1787)

491. Died: Last Saturday John Pettigrow, of Kittery, drowned in Portsmouth Harbor on his return from Newburyport. He leaves a wife and two children. (3,122 4/18/1787)

492. Col. John Dennett orders Commanding Officers of the companies of the first New Hampshire regiment of the militia to gather their men early on Monday to ensure they can form on Downing Plain by 10 A. M. Portsmouth, April 18, 1787. (3,122 4/18/1787)

493. As per the Capt. General's orders, the first regiment of foot under Col. Dennett, the corps of independent light horse, commanded by Col. Wentworth, several corps of light horse under Col. Cogswell, the alarm companies commanded by Col. Gains, Col. Whipple and Col. Hill and the company of artillery commanded by Capt. Woodward assembled for review on Downing's Plain. The Capt. General and Chief Justice Livermore reviewed the assembled troops. (3,123 4/26/1787)

494. Samuel Storer has moved his shop to Fore Street on Spring Hill near the market. There he has English hardware and West India goods for sale. (3,123 4/26/1787)

495. All persons with demands on the estate of John Tibbets, late of Dover, deceased, are asked to present their demands to Lydia Tibbetts, Administratrix, for prompt settlement. Dover, April, 24, 1787. (3,123 4/26/1787)

496. Elizabeth Butler advises the ladies of Portsmouth that she is in business to make mantuas and offers her services to the

ladies. She has been trained in the trade while in Boston. (3,123 4/26/1787)

497. John Sullivan, Capt. General, has canceled all reviews except the one for the 18th regiment. Durham, April 27, 1787. (3,124 5/3/1787)

498. James McHard reports that his barn was broken into on April 1, and his horse was stolen. His horse is eight years old, fourteen hands high, with a small white spot on its forehead. A handsome reward will be paid for the return of the horse. Hopkinton, April 11, 1787. (3,124 5/3/1787)

499. Four indents were lost in Portsmouth on April 26. Three were signed by J. Hardy and one by Michael Hillegas. They were wrapped in paper with a note saying Isaac Frye's certificates. A handsome reward will be given to the person returning them to the printer. (3,124 5/3/1787)

500. N. Rouselet is selling West India goods from his grocery store, which was formerly occupied by William Knight, on Back Street. (3,124 5/3/1787)

501. Ship News:

		ENTERED FROM
Brig *Endeavour*	Riley	L'Orient
Schooner *Polly*	Boadge	Martinico
Brig *Nancy*	Frost	Trinadad
Brig *Abigail*	Peirce	Port-au-Prince

(3,125 5/10/1787)

502. On May 1, a person or persons broke on to the Portsmouth town pound and released two horses of Nathaniel S. Griffith, which were legally impounded. The selectmen will pay a reward of $8 for evidence which will lead to the conviction of the perpetrators. (3,125 5/10/1787)

503. Ship News

		ENTERED FROM
Sloop *Randolph*	Gardner	Philadelphia
Brig *Dover*	Manning	St. Eustatia

CLEARED FOR
Brig *Astrea*   Salter   West Indies
Brig *Polly*   Rice   West Indies
(3,125 5/10/1787)

504. On May 12, 1787, the following people had letters at the Portsmouth post office:

•A: Capt. Richard Adams, Londonderry
•B: Joseph Bass, Portsmouth; Zephaniah Butler, Nottingham; Henry Belden, Portsmouth; Isaac Blaisdell, New Salisbury; Jonathan Blake, Kingston; Moses Barnett, Londonderry; Robert Barrley, Londonderry; Charles Barrett, New Ipswich; Benjamin Butler, Nottingham; James Butler, Portsmouth
•C: John Call, Exeter; Enoch Clark, Greenland; Thomas Cogswell, Gilmanton; Joshua Cortiss, Hampstead; Dr. Edward Creemore, New Castle; General Cilley Nottingham; Joseph Collins, New Marlboro; David Copps, Wakefield; James Carruth, Kingston; George Calder, Portsmouth
•D: Michael Dwyer, New Holderness; James Deady (2), Peterborough; Benjamin Dearborn, Portsmouth
•F: William Furnell, Portsmouth
•G: Nathaniel S. Griffith, Portsmouth; Abigail Gail, Kingston; Nabby Gay, Heasdale; Robert Gray, Dover; Nancy Gage, Dover; John Grant, Berwick
•H: Patty Haslet, Portsmouth; Gilbert Horney, Portsmouth; John Haggens, Portsmouth; Robert Harrold, Portsmouth; Philip Harty, Berwick; Oliver Heasleng, Charlestown; Enoch Hoag, Dover; Stephen Heath, Lebanon
•J: Elijah Jenkins, Berwick
•K: Levi Kendell, Sanford
•L: John Lane, Portsmouth
•M: William Moore, Kittery; Clement March, Greenland; Valentine Mathis, Durham
•N: Henry Nutter, Portsmouth
•O: Robert Oram, Portsmouth; Abigail Odiorne, Madbury; William Odiorne, Newmarket
•P: Mehitable Prelley, Portsmouth; Stephen Parker, Durham; Betsy Pynchon, Hampton; George Poore, Portsmouth; Francis

Pearse, Towow; Amos Peaslee, Dover; Edward Park, Portsmouth

•R: David Ricker, Somersworth; Bostwick Ruggles, Portsmouth; Susey Rollens, Deerfield

•S: Christopher Strickland, Portsmouth; Edward Sergent, Portsmouth; Amos Shefford, Peterborough; Joseph Smith, Portsmouth

•T: Henry Trefethen, New Castle

•W: John Wendell (3), Portsmouth

•Rev. John Wheelock, Dartmouth

•Jeremiah Wilie, Durham

•Andrew Wiggins, Stratham

•Ebenezer Waldin, Dover

(3,126, 5/17/1787)

505. John Tufton Mason and his wife Mary, formerly of Portsmouth and now residing in Buckden, England, have hired Thomas Martin, an attorney, to handle all their affairs in the United States. This includes dealings relating to their mansion and property both in Portsmouth and throughout New Hampshire. Portsmouth, May 19, 1787. (3,127 5/24/1787)

506. Boardman & Son have linseed oil, snuff, chocolate and tobacco for sale. (3,127 5/24/1787)

507. Stephen Peabody, Clerk of the Convention, reminds all ministers that at the Convention of Ministers on June 2, 1786 at Concord, they agree to have the Election Sermon presented on the first Wednesday of June 1787. All clergy are urged to attend. Atkinson, May 14, 1787. (3,127 5/24/1787)

508. Samuel Hill has pot ash kettles and coolers for pot ash for sale. (3,129 6/7/1787)

509. On June 6, the General Court of New Hampshire met in Concord. Members selected John Sparhawk as Speaker and John Calfe as Clerk of the House of Representatives. Final vote for President was as follows:

John Sullivan   3642

(Voting results)

John Langdon	4034
Samuel Livermore	603
Joshua Bartlett	628
Others	378

Thus there was no majority from the voters. Vacancies in the Senate were filled as follows:

Rockingham County
  George Atkinson
  Joshua Wentworth
  Joseph Gilman
  John Bell
  Peter Green
Strafford County
  Ebenezer Thompson
  Ebenezer Smith
Hillsborough County
  Robert Means
  Joshua Bayley
Cheshire County
  John Bellows
  Amos Shepard
Grafton County
  Elisha Payne
(3,130 6/14/1787)

510. Died: At Portsmouth, Daniel Fowle, 72, last Friday. (3,130 6/14/1787)

511. Ship News:

		ENTERED FROM
Brig *Tom*	Baggs	Jamaica
		CLEARED FOR
Brig *Abigail*	Pierce	West Indies
Brig *Dover*	Manning	West Indies
Schooner *Betsy*	Salter	West Indies
Sloop *Mary*	Hooper	West Indies
Schooner *Eliza*	Gunnison	West Indies

(3,130 6/14/1787)

512.   John Langdon, John Pickering, Nicholas Gilman and Benjamin Bellows have been selected by the General Court to represent New Hampshire in Congress. (3,132 6/28/1787)

513.   Job Shattuck, noted rebel, is to be executed at Concord, MA today. (3,132 6/28/1787)

514.   Ship News:

		ENTERED FROM
Brig *Viscompt d'Arrott*	Mendum	Tobago
Brig *Sophia*	Roberts	l'Orient
Sloop *Catharine*	Atkins	Shelburne
Schooner *Blossom*	Trundy	Demerara
		CLEARED FOR
Sloop *Catharine*	Atkins	Shelburne

(3,132 6/28/1787)

515.   A few good shipping horses are wanted for purchase. Enquire at Nathaniel Folsom's store in Portsmouth. (3,132 6/28/1787)

516.   Daniel Symes has a new assortment of goods for sale at his shop on Congress Street, Portsmouth. (3,132 6/28/1787)

517.   A few good shipping horses are wanted for purchase. Enquire at Nathaniel Folsom's store in Portsmouth. (3,132 6/28/1787)

518.   Daniel Symes has a new assortment of goods for sale at his shop on Congress Street, Portsmouth. (3,132 6/28/1787)

519.   Yesterday a number of men celebrated the eleventh anniversary of American Independence by assembling at the coffee house tavern in Portsmouth. They were honored by the presence of President Sullivan and Judge Langdon.   Col. Wentworth's Independent Light Horse and Capt. Woodward's performed military maneuvers on the parade in the morning. (3,133 7/5/1787)

520. Died: At Portsmouth, Mrs. Hannah Sherburne, widow, relict of Ephraim Sherburne, late of Portsmouth. (3,133 7/5/1787)

521. Richard Wentworth, apprentice, ran away from Samuel Chapman. A three pence reward will be paid for his return. Wakefield, May 5, 1787. (3,133 7/5/1787)

522. Last Monday, John Langdon, a member of the Congress from New Hampshire, left Portsmouth for Philadelphia where the Congress will meet. (3,134 7/12/1787)

523. Ship News:

		ENTERED FROM
Schooner *Nancy*	Brown	Demerara
Brig *Dauphin*	Cutts	St. Domingo
Brig *John*	Yeaton	Maryland
Brig *Betsey*	Hall	Nantez
		CLEARED FOR
Brig *Carbonear*	Briard	West Indies
Schooner *Swallow*	Mountford	St. Peters
Brig *Dispatch*	Wingate	W. Indies

(3,134 7/12/1787)

524. Joseph White and Joshua Pike, Collectors, announce that the following persons have not paid their parish taxes on their pews in the North Meeting House:
John Ayers
Mrs. Sarah Russell
Heirs of Hen. Sherburne
Daniel Hart
Henry Sherburne
Heirs of J. Stoodley
Widow Mayo
Joseph Walker
Charles Roberts
Heirs of J. Seaward
Heirs of J. Simpson
Heirs of Rich. Towle
Isaac Tucker

Pews will be sold on July 30 if parish taxes have not been paid by then. Portsmouth, July 9, 1787. (3,134 7/12/1787)

525. Stephen Page informs the public that his son has a £165 note against him dated June 1769. This note is a forgery and Stephen will not pay it. Hampton, July 16, 1787. (3,135 7/19/1787)

526.   Ship News:

		ENTERED FROM
Sloop *Sally*	Smith	St. Martins
		CLEARED FOR
Sloop *Endeavour*	Longer	West Indies

(3,135 7/19/1787)

527. John Sullivan, via Gen. orders, asks Maj. Gen. Cilley and Maj. Gen. Bellows to create a review schedule for their brigades for the fall. Durham, July 16, 1787. (3,136 7/26/1787)

528. On July 18, two green swivels, which were properly mounted, were stolen from the ship *Elizabeth*. A two dollar reward will be given for their return by Joseph Seaward. July 23, 1787. (3,136 7/26/1787)

529. Property of Jonathan Moulton of Hampton has been advertised for sale in Scotland and Ireland. The land on Moultonborough Neck has been sold to some men from Scotland. They will arrive next spring. They plan to carry out manufacturing. As part of the payment, Dr. McNorton has sent a large amount of Dr. Anderson's famous Scotch pills to Moulton as partial payment. They are for sale at Moulton's stores in Dover and Hampton. (3,136 7/26/1787)

530. Ship News: On July 6, brig *Carbonear* sailed from Portsmouth to the West Indies with a load of lumber. On July 14 the brig sprung a leak at 36° 40′ N and 65° W. The pumps could not keep up and the brig was filled with water on July 17. At that time the captain and crew were rescued by sloop *Nabby*, of New London, Capt. Coit, which was bound for Cape Francois. The next day the captain and crew of the *Carbonear*

were transferred to the brig *Dispatch*, Capt. Wingate, of Portsmouth. The *Dispatch* was en route the West Indies. On July 20 the *Dispatch* was thrown on her beam's end in a violent squall. All the hay on deck was lost and the *Dispatch* had to alter course for Portsmouth. The *Dispatch* arrived there last Saturday. (3,137 8/2/1787)

531. Ship News:

		ENTERED FROM
Brig *Irish Gimblet*	Turner	Martinico
Ship *Atlantic*	Trefethen	Cape Francois
Schooner *Mary*	Frost	Cape Francois
		CLEARED FOR
Brig *Nancy*	York	Great Britain
Brig *Mary Ann*	Gerrish	West Indies
Brig *Sophia*	Orn	Great Britain

(3,137 8/2/1787)

532. Joseph Champney has an assortment of clothes and cloth for sale, at his store opposite the post office, which was imported on the last ship from London. Portsmouth, August 1, 1787. (3,137 8/2/1787)

533. Ship News: Last Sunday, Capt. Thomas Rice arrived in Portsmouth on a brig which had sailed from Dominica in 17 days. On July 28 he had spoken to ship *Hope*, James McGee, from Canton, China en route New York. They had been at sea 183 days. All was well. (3,138 8/9/1787)

534. Last Monday night several villains broke into the store of Nathaniel Folsom, merchant, and stole five hundred dollars worth of goods. (3,139 8/16/1787)

535. Sundry articles saved from the brig *Carbonear* will be sold at public vendue. The sale will take place on August 24 at the store of Capt. Samuel Gerrish. (3,139 8/16/1787)

536. N. Folsom and E. Hall are offering a thirty dollar reward to whoever discovers the thieves that broke into the Folsom

store. Portsmouth, August 15, 1787. (3,139 8/16/1787)

537. All persons having demands on the estate of Daniel Jackson, late of Portsmouth, deceased, are asked to settle promptly with Benjamin Chandler, Administrator. Portsmouth, August 10, 1787. (3,139 8/16/1787)

538. Died: At Portsmouth, Noah Parker, 52; Charles Blunt, 48; Mrs. Phebe Ayrs, 20, daughter of Jonathan Ayrs; a child of Thomas Sherburne; Jacob Treadwell, 51. (3,149 8/23/1787)

539. Ship News:

		ENTERED FROM
Schooner *Industry*	Currier	St. Eustatia
Brig *Hero*	Edwards	Martinico
Sloop *Dolphin*	Coffin	St. Bartholomew
Schooner *Betsey*	Salter	St. Bartholomew
		CLEARED FOR
Schooner *Polly*	White	West Indies
Brig *Betsey*	Hall	West Indies
Ship *Xeppel*	Young	Cape Francois

(3,140 8/23/1787)

540. Public notice is given that a petition has been preferred to the Gen. Court of New Hampshire by Sarson Belcher of Boston, MA on his behalf and the behalf of the proprietors and land owners of Peterborough, NH. It sets forth that in June 1738 a grant of land was made to certain persons by the Gen. Court of Massachusetts which empowered Jonathan Prescott to call a meeting of the proprietors. This was done. The town was laid out and settled according to the results of that meeting. In 1748 the proprietors of the Mason Patent released their rights to this land. These actions were recorded in the book of the Gen. Court of Massachusetts. As these books were destroyed by fire, that the case to confirm this action will be heard on the third Wednesday of the next session. Attested to by Joseph Pearson, Secr'y, Exeter, August 16, 1787. (3,140 8/23/1787)

541. All persons having claims against the estate of David Cullam, late of Portsmouth, mariner, deceased, are requested to

present same to Margaret Cullam, Administratrix, for settlement. Portsmouth, August 22, 1787. (3,140 8/23/1787)

542. Ship News: Last Tuesday the brig *Izette*, Capt. Drisco, arrived in 64 days from Liverpool. Capt. Drisco left Capt. Pearse and Capt. Horney, both of Portsmouth, in Liverpool. (3,141 8/30/1787)

543. Ship News:

		ENTERED FROM
Schooner *Success*	Jackson	St. Eustatia
Brig *Cooper*	Sellars	Demerara
Schooner *Fanny*	Daigee	Hispaniola
Brig *Dover*	Manning	Cape Francois
Brig *Endeavor*	Riley	Cape Francois
Brig *David*	Parrot	St. Bartholomew
Brig *Astrea*	Salter	Cape Francois
Brig *Two Sisters*	----	St. Lucia
Brig *Izette*	Drisco	Liverpool

(3,141 8/30/1787)

544. Died: At Portsmouth, Mrs. Mary Mutchemore, 51, wife Capt. Joseph Mutchemore, of Portsmouth; a child of Joseph Trickey; and a child of William Sowersby. (3,141 9/13/1787)

545. Ship News:

		ENTERED FROM
Sloop *Henrietta*	Whitney	St. Martin's
Sloop *Cripple*	Hollister	New York

(3,141 9/13/1787)

546. All those who have sold exciseable liquors in Strafford County from October 1, 1786 to October 1, 1787 are to settle their tax accounts with Thomas Cogswell, Collector of Excise at his home in Gilmantown or with Col. Amos Cogswell in Dover before October 10. Gilmantown, August 30, 1787. (3,141 9/13/1787)

547. Ship News:

		ENTERED FROM
Brig *Randolph*	Gardner	St. Martins
Schooner *Eliza*	Gunison	St. Eustatia

		CLEARED FOR
Brig *Endeavour*	Briard	West Indies
(3,142 9/20/1787)		

548. Copies of the sermon delivered by Rev. Mr. Buckminster before the Gen. Assembly of New Hampshire last June are for sale at office of the printer of this newspaper.
(3,145 9/27/1787)

549. Ship News:

Brig *Lovely Lass*	Newby	ENTERED FROM Newfoundland
Brig *Mary*	Pile	Great Britain
Schooner *Polly*	Boadge	Martinico
Brig *Nancy*	Frost	Port-au-Prince
		CLEARED FOR
Brig *David*	Parrot	Martinico
Brig *Elizabeth*	Lang	West Indies
Ship *Elizabeth*	Seaward	Bristol
(3,145 9/27/1787)		

550. Jona. Rawson, Aid-de-Camp to the Commander in Chief, orders all officers of the New Hampshire First Brigade to appear on September 30 in their respective parishes in uniform with a black ribbon on their left arm in respect for their late Brigadier Gen.. (3,145 9/27/1787)

551. Supply Clap has a 3,800 acre tract of land for sale in whole or lots of 200 acres. The land was granted to Thomas Gray and is in the northwest corner of Conway. The Saco River and the Ellis River run through the property as does the great road from the Upper Cohoss. It is about sixty miles from Dover landing. Portsmouth, September 25, 1787.
(3,145 9/27/1787)

552. On September 17, 1787 the proposed Constitution of the United States was passed by the Federal Convention. John Langdon and Nicholas Gilman signed for New Hampshire and Nathaniel Gorham and Rufus King signed for Massachusetts.
(3,146 10/4/1787)

553. Col. Gains reports that the Gen. Court of New Hampshire concluded its session at Charleston last Saturday. (3,146 10/4/1787)

554. Samuel Hutchins has a large two story house for sale. It is located a half mile from Dr. Haven's meeting house and is adjacent to Capt. William Fernald's property. (3,146 10/4/1787)

555. Abner Blasdel has the best quality Georges' stone lime for sale. (3,146 10/4/1787)

556. A pair of oxen, owned by Daniel Newcomb of Keene, were killed in Gilsom when a tree fell on them. This was the result of a major rain storm that hit the area. (3,147 10/11/1787)

557. Ship News:

		ENTERED FROM
Brig *Three Brothers*	Sherburne	St. Lucia
Sloop *Mary*	Hooper	Tobago
Brig *Kitty*	Thompson	London
		CLEARED FOR
Brig *Olive*	Smallcorn	West Indies
Ship *Mary*	Tilestone	Great Britain
Brig *Randolph*	Thompson	W. Indies

(3,147 10/11/1787)

558. On November 15 an auction will be held at Dearborn's Auction Room. One large family Bible, an assortment of other book and sundry articles of drugs and medicine will be for sale. Portsmouth, October 8, 1787. (3,147 10/11/1787)

559. Betty Hickey, living in Portsmouth, has 500 acres of land in the southeast part of Lempster for sale. This land has a mill stream running through it, has 30 cleared acres and has a new barn. (3,147 10/11/1787)

560. Sewell's Almanack for 1788 is now at press. (3,147 10/11/1787)

561. George S. Homans has moved his tailor business from Pitt Street to the corner house on Water Street, which is at the head of Col. Sherburne's wharf. (3,147 10/11/1787)

562. All persons with claims on George Doig, of Portsmouth, painter, are requested to settle them so he may close his accounts as quickly as possible. (3,147 10/11/1787)

563. A gentleman from Londonderry reports that Maj. Gen. Cilley was escorted from Chester to Londonderry on October 1 by a large contingent of men. On October 2 he reviewed the 8th regiment of infantry, commanded by Col. Runnels, and a company of cavalry, commanded by Capt. Hunter. Then these forces performed some maneuvers before Gen. Cilley and Gen. Reid. The following day the Gen.s were escorted back to Chester by Capt. Preston and his company of cavalry. There Gen. Cilley reviewed the 17th regiment of infantry, commanded by Col. Emerson, and a company of cavalry, commanded by Capt. Preston.   Later Gen. Reid led the forces in several maneuvers which resulted in loud applause from the spectators. (3,148 11/18/1787)

564. Ship News:		ENTERED FROM
Schooner *Success*	Jackson	St. Peter's
Sloop *Sally*	Parker	Philadelphia
		CLEARED FOR
Ship *George & Sally*	Mountford	Britain
Brig *Mary*	Pile	Britain
Ship *Three Sisters*	Palmer	St. Vincent
(3,148 10/18/1787)		

565. Died: Last Saturday at Portsmouth, John Sparhawk, 45, merchant, late speaker of the Gen. Court of New Hampshire, and elder of the Sandamanian Society of Portsmouth. His body was laid to rest on Sunday in the burying ground of the Queen's Chapel. (3,145 10/27/1787)

566. All persons with accounts outstanding with the estate of Enoch Merrill, late of Stratham, deceased, are asked to present

same to Joseph Merrill, Executor to the Estate.   Stratham, October 25, 1787. (3,145 10/27/1787)

567.   Died: At Portsmouth, Samuel Jones, 45, of Portsmouth. (3,150 11/1/1787)

568.   Ship News:

		ENTERED FROM
Ship *Admiral Parker*	Skinner	London
Ship *Polly*	Nixon	London
Ship *Ann*	Grave	London
Sloop *Endeavor*	Louger	Tobago
Sloop *Mary*	Fernald	Cape Francois
Schooner *Blosom*	Haven	Madeira
		CLEARED FOR
Schooner *Swallow*	Palmer	S. Carolina
Brig *Lovely Lass*	Newby	Barbados

(3,150 11/1/1787)

569.   John Fennex, 18, an indented servant, has run away from John Talton.   People are cautioned against harboring this runaway.   New Castle, November 1, 1787. (3,150 11/1/1787)

570.   Ship News:

		ENTERED FROM
Sloop *John*	Yeaton	Philadelphia
Brig *Molly*	Gunison	Barbados
		CLEARED FOR
Brig *Polly*	Rice	Great Britain
Brig *Astrea*	Salter	West Indies (3,151

11/9/1787)

571.   Died: At Portsmouth, Joseph Moulton, 77; Capt. Edmund Roberts, 42; and a child of George Turner. (3,152 11/16/1787)

572.   Ship News:

		ENTERED FROM
Snow *Nine Sons*	Briard	Cape Francois
Brig *Montpellier*	Miller	Tobago
Ship *William*	Pearse	London
		CLEARED FOR
Brig *Nancy*	Brown	Maderia

Sloop *Sally*   Flagg   Maderia
(3,152 11/16/1787)

573. John Sullivan, Captain Gen., sent out a general order congratulating all regiments for their fine performances at the reviews each has had with the Commander in Chief. He singled out Maj. Gen. Cilley and Brig. Gen. Bartlett for their excellent leadership. Durham, November 12, 1787. (3,152 11/16/1787)

574. The following men should contact James Gooch to collect the balances due them for serving on the Continental ships Boston, Alliance and Ranger:
Charles Ricker
James Holbrook
Abner Coffin
Joseph Roberts
William Hilton
Chance Wentworth
Lt. Richard Furber Jr.
Nathaniel Pike
Portsmouth, November 12, 1787. (3,152 11/16/1787)

575. Sewell's Almanack for 1788 is now for sale at Gerrish's printing office on Congress Street. (3,153 11/23/1787)

576. Daniel Humphreys has a large quantity of printing paper and other types of paper, which he just received by ship from London, for sale at his home on Pleasant Street, near the South Meeting House. Portsmouth, November 1, 1787. (3,153 11/23/1787)

577. The Commanding Gen. praises Maj. Gen. Bellows and Brig. Gen. Blanchard for reviewing the fifth, ninth and twelfth regiments of the militia. Durham, November 24, 1787. (3,154 12/4/1787)

578. Died: At Portsmouth, Mrs. Dorothy Reed, 74, widow, relict of Capt. Philip Reed, of Portsmouth; Mrs. Sarah Sherburne, 35, comfort of Capt. Benjamin Sherburne; a child of George

Walden; and Samuel Waters, 54. (3,156 12/18/1787)

579. Col. Samuel Ham has the hull of a new 190 ton, double decked vessel for sale. It is now lying on Ham's beach. Portsmouth, December 18, 1787. (3,156 12/18/1787)

580. All persons with accounts with the estate of Francis Mussuaw, late of Portsmouth, mariner, deceased, are asked to present same to Alice Mussuaw, Administratrix. (3,156 12/18/1787)

581. Ship News:

		CLEARED FOR
Schooner *Betsy*	Salter	West Indies
Brig *Nancy*	Frost	West Indies
Brig *Mary Ann*	Gerrish	West Indies
Ship *William*	Pearse	West Indies

(3,157 12/26/1787)

582. Samuel Bean, post rider, has contracted to ride the mail once a week between Portsmouth and Concord via Exeter and Haverhill. Bean stays at Col. Brewster's Coffee House Tavern in Portsmouth. December 21, 1787. (3,157 12/26/1787)

583. Woodbury Langdon, Daniel Rindge and John Parker have been appointed Commissioners to the Estate of John Moffatt, late of Portsmouth, deceased, represented insolvent. They will conduct business at the home of Col. William Brewster, in, Portsmouth on the last Monday of the next six months. Portsmouth, December 20, 1787. (3,157 12/26/1787)

584. Ship News:

		ENTERED FROM
Schooner *Mary*	Prescot	St. Eustatia
		CLEARED FOR
Brig *Tryall*	Sargent	West Indies
Brig *Betsey*	Long	West Indies
Brig *Abigail*	Pierce	West Indies

(3,158 1/2/1788)

585. Ship News: ENTERED FROM
Brig *Olive*   Smallcorn   Tobago
                                         CLEARED FOR
Brig *Hero*   Edwards   Ireland
(3,159 1/9/1788)

586. Ship News: ENTERED FROM
Brig *Elizabeth*   Lang   Port au Prince
Brig *Randolph*   Gardner   St. Thomas
Ship *Keppel*   Young   Cape Francois
                                         CLEARED FOR
Brig *Susannah*   Parker   West Indies
Brig *Olive*   Smallcorn   West Indies
(3,161 1/23/1788)

587. Samuel Sherburne Jr., Attorney to the Administrator, asks all persons with accounts outstanding to the estate of Ebenezer Jackson, late of Portsmouth, mariner, deceased, to contact him at his office in Portsmouth to settle their claims. January 22, 1788. (3,161 1/23/1788)

588. A public vendue will be held January 24 at Mrs. Purcell's to sell the real estate, except for the widow's thirds, of Elisha Briard, late of Portsmouth, deceased. January 7, 1788. (3,161 1/23/1788)

589. Benjamin Dearborn, Attorney to the Administratrix, informs the public that, by license issued by Phillips White, Judge of Probate of Wills, etc. for Rockingham County, an auction will be held February 28, on the premises, to sell the house and land of Joseph Holbrook, late of Portsmouth, deceased, except for the widow's dower. Portsmouth, January 28, 1788. (3,162 1/30/1788)

590. Any person willing and able to provide 2,200 pounds of beef, 1,200 pounds of flour and seven bushels of peas for the rations of Capt. Salter's Company, stationed at the Fort are to contact Supply Clap, Commissary Gen.. Portsmouth, January 30, 1788. (3,162 1/30/1788)

591. Keith Spence has a consignment of English goods for sale at his store, lately occupied by Capt. Martin, on Market Street. Portsmouth, February 6, 1788. (3,163 2/6/1788)

592. The Convention of New Hampshire assembled at Exeter last Wednesday. On February 13, Josiah Bartlett was selected Chairman of the Convention. Samuel Livermore, John Taylor Gilman and Benjamin West were selected to examine the returns of the members. On February 14, John Calfe was elected Secretary and John Sullivan was elected President. (3,165, 2/20/1788)

593. Ship News: Last Friday the schooner *Dove*, Capt. Tredick, arrived at New Castle in 18 days from St. Eustatia. Left there was Capt. Hooper in a sloop from Portsmouth. Capt. Appleton sailed from Portsmouth, some time ago, en route Charleston, SC. He ran into such foul weather that he had to divert to Martinico, where he arrived safely. The brig *David*, Capt. Parrott, from Portsmouth, was blown off course and arrived in St. Bartholomew. Capt. Chauncy arrived in St. Lucia in a schooner from Kittery. Captains Drisco and Jackson, from Portsmouth, have arrived in Martinico. (3,165 2/20/1788)

594. Joshua Wentworth has a variety of goods for sale at his store that is near his house. (3,165 2/20/1788)

595. Members of the New Hampshire Convention and the towns they represent are as follows:

Portsmouth	John Langdon
	Pierce Long
	John Pickering
Exeter	John T. Gilman
Londonderry	Col. Daniel Runnels
	Archibald McMurphy
Chester	Joseph Blanchard
Newington	Mr. Adams
Greenland	Dr. Ichabod Weeks
Rye	Nathan Goss

(Members of the New Hampshire Convention)

New Castle	Henry Prescott
North Hampton	Rev. Mr. Thurston
Hampton	Christopher Toppan
Hampton Falls & Seabrook	Rev. Dr. Langdon
Stratham	Jonathan Wiggin
Kensington	Jeremiah Fogg
South Hampton & East Kingstown	Benjamin Clough
Kingstown	Josiah Bartlett
Brintwood	Dr. Thomas Stowe Ranney
Epping	Nathaniel Ladd
Newmarket	Col. Rogers
Nottingham	Gen. Thomas Bartlett
Deerfield	Dr. E. Chadwick
Northwood, Epsom & Allenstown	James Gray
Chichester & Pittsfield	Benjamin Sias
Canterbury	Col. Jeremiah Clough
Northfield	Charles Glidden
Loudon	Jonathan Smith
Concord	Capt. Benjamin Emery
Pembrook	Samuel Daniels
Candia	Stephen Fifield
Raymond & Poplin	Thomas Chase
Hawke & Sandown	Nehemiah Sleeper
Hampstead	John Calfe
Atkinson & Plastow	Col. Benjamin Stone
Salem	Lt. Thomas Dow
Newtown	Capt. Robert Steward
Wyndham	James Betten
Pelham	Rev. Mr. Amos Moody
Dover	Dr. Ezra Green
Durham	Hon. John Sullivan
Somersworth	Dr. Moses Carr
Rochester	Barnabas Palmer
Barrington	Samuel Hale
Sandborntown	William Harper
Gilmantown	Gen. Badger
Lee	Capt. Reuben Hill

(Members of the New Hampshire Convention)

Madbury	Rev. William Hooper
Meredith & New Hampton	Col. Ebenezer Smith
Sandwich & Tamworth	D. Bedee
Moultonborough, Tuftonborough, Wolfborough & Ossipee	Nathaniel Shannon
Conway, Eaton, Burton & Lucatiens	David Page
Barnstead, New Durham, & New Durham Gore	Jonathan Chesley
Wakefield, Middletown & Effingham	Nicholas Austin
Litchfield & Derryfield	Capt. Daniel Bixby
Dunstable	Deacon William Hunt
Merrimack	T. Taylor
Bedford	Stephen Dole
Goffstown	William Page
Hollis	Lt. Daniel Kindrick
Amherst	Mr. Atherton
Raby & Mason	Amos Dakin
New Ipswich	Capt. Charles Bartlett
Wilton	William Abbot
Lynborough	Benjamin Jones
Temple & Peterborough Slip	John Cragin
Peterborough & Society Land	Maj. Nathaniel Dix
Hancock, Antrim & Dearing	Evan Dow
Henniker & Hillsborough	Lt. Robert B. Wilkens
New Boston	John Cockran
Weare	John Dow
Hopkinton	Joshua Morse
Dunbarton & Bow	Capt. Jacob Green
Fishersfield, Sutton & Warner	Nathan Bean
Charlestown	Benjamin West
Alstead	Capt. Oliver Sheppard
Keene	Rev. Mr. Hall
Swanzey Maj.	Elisha Whitcomb
Richmond	Jonathan Gaskill
Jaffrey	Abel Parker

(Members of the New Hampshire Convention)

Winchester	Moses Chamberlain
Westmoreland	Archelaus Temple
Chesterfield	Soloman Harvey
Rindge	Capt. O. Thomas
Walpole	Gen. Benjamin Bellows
	Aaron Allen
Claremont	Matthias Storie
Cornish & Grantham	John Chase
Acworth, Lemster & Marlow	Daniel Grout
Surry & Gilsom	Col. Jonathan Smith
Stoddard & Washington	Thomas Penniman
Dublin & Packersfield	Sam. Griffin
Marlborough	Jedediah Tainter
Fitzwilliam	Caleb Winch
Plainfield	Maj. Joseph Kimball
Proteckworth & Hinsdale	Uriah Evans
Holderness, Compton & Thornton	Judge Livermore
Plymouth, Rumney & Wentworth	Francis Worster
New Chester, Alexandria &	
Cockermouth	Mr. Crawford
Enfield, Canaan, Cardigan,	
Dorchester & Grafton	Jesse Johnson
Hanover	Jonathan Freeman
Lebanon	Capt. David Hough
Lyme & Orford	Col. William Simpson
Haverhill, Piermont, Warren,	
Coventry, Lincoln & Franconia	Col. Joseph Hutchins
Bath, Lyman, Landaff, Concord,	
Littleton & Dalton	Maj. Stephen Young
Lancaster, Northumberland,	
Stratford, Dartmouth, Piercy,	
Cockburne & Coleburn	Capt. John Weeks

(3,166 2/27/1788)

596.   Died: At Portsmouth, George Atkinson, 54; Mrs. Margaret Wentworth, 78, relict of Hunking Wentworth; and George Waters, 48. (3,166 2/27/1788)

597. Ship News: CLEARED FOR
Brig *Patty Wentworth*   Wardrobe   West Indies
Sloop *Catharine*   Gerrish   West Indies
(3,166 2/27/1788)

598. Thomas Bartlett, Dudley Odlin and Amos Gale, Committee, announce that the excise on spiritous liquors for Rockingham County, running from October 1, 1787 to October 1, 1788, will be sold at public vendue at the home of Benjamin Lamson, innholder in Exeter, on March 13. (3,166 2/27/1788)

599. Results of voting for President of New Hampshire and Senators are as follows:

Concord:
  President
John Langdon   107
Peter Green   35
President Sullivan   3

  Senators
John Bell   88
Peter Green   78
John Pickering   54
John Sherburne   32
Joshua Wentworth   31
Peirce Long   28
Nathaniel Peabody   36
Christopher Toppan   29

Londonderry:
  President
John Langdon   103
Matthew Thornton   5
Samuel Livermore   3
President Sullivan   1

Hopkington, Boscawan, Bow and Northfield voted almost unanimously for John Langdon for President. (3,167 3/12/1788)

600. Died: At York about three weeks ago, Mrs. Elizabeth Rayns, 100. (3,167 3/12/1788)

601. Mrs. Homans will open a school at her home on Water Street, at the head of Col. Sherburn's wharf, on the first Wednesday in April. She will teach needle work, reading, etc. (3,167 3/12/1788)

602. Sarah Moulton and Thomas Leavitt, Executors, ask all persons with claims on the estate of Gen. Jonathan Moulton, late of Hampton, deceased, to present the same. Hampton, February 9, 1788. (3,167 3/12/1788)

603. The editor of the *Mercury*, Robert Gerrish, notes that only a few of his customers have paid their bills. This is not enough to even cover the cost of the paper. No further mention is made that this will be the final issue. (3,167 3/12/1788)

INDEX

Note: The number following each name indicates the abstract within which it can be found.

A

ABBOT
John, 413; Mrs.
Elizabeth, 317; William,
419, 595.

ADAMS
40, 112, 157; Capt.
Richard, 504; Ephraim,
122; Jonathan, 419;
Josiah, 196, 320, 419;
Mr., 55, 595; Nath., 22;
Nathaniel, 76, 286, 419,
482.

AIKEN
James, 419; Nenien,
419.

AINSWORTH
Lab., 439.

AKERMAN
Nahum, 482; Walter,
76, 286, 482.

AKIN
John, 183.

ALDRICH
G., 428.

ALEXANDER
Reuben, 421, 425.

ALLEN
512; Aaron, 595; John,
419; Jonathan, 149;
Joseph, 167, 171; Mr.,
177; Samuel, 313, 314,
315.

AMAZEEN
14, 77.

AMBROSE
Capt. Nathaniel, 338;
Samuel, 439.

AMEE
Ellis, 406.

AMES
421; Stephen, 338.

ANDERSON
Dr., 529.

ANDREWS
26; Isaac, 419; Katty,
406.

ANNIN
David, 439.

APPLETON
Capt., 592; William, 79,
100.

ARNOLD
Jonathan, 421.

ASHLEY
  Capt. Daniel, 338;
  Daniel, 425; Oliver, 421;
  Samuel, 419, 421, 425.
ATHERTON
  Joshua, 89, 437; Mr.,
  594.
ATKINS
  516; John, 406.
ATKINSON
  George, 54, 122, 279,
  286, 332, 419, 466, 475,
  509, 596; Miles, 197;
  Samuel, 428; Theodore,
  186, 188, 263; Theodore
  Jr., 186, 188, 263.
AUCHMUTY
  Robert, 263.
AUSTIN
  Nicholas, 595.
AYER/AYERS/AIR
  Capt. John, 370; John,
  183, 524; Jonathan, 538;
  Mrs. Phebe, 538;
  Perkins, 76, 286, 482;
  William, 421.

B
BADGER
  Col. Joseph, 122, 338;
  Gen., 595; Joseph, 356,
  419; Joseph Jr., 419, 425.
BAGGS
  511.
BAILEY
  Abner, 439; Joshua, 419;
  Mary, 251; William,
  251.

BAKER
  Moses, 421, 425; Otis,
  122, 332, 419; Samuel,
  196, 320; Thomas, 421.
BALCH
  Benjamin, 439.
BALDWIN
  Thomas, 439.
BALL
  Mrs. Mary, 485.
BARKER
  Barnabas, 278; Enoch,
  117; Stephen, 333.
BARLLEY/BARRLEY
  Robert, 406, 504.
BARNARD
  Jeremiah, 439; Moses,
  122.
BARNES/BARNS
  Jonathan, 439; Joseph,
  38.
BARNETT
  Moses, 406, 504.
BARR
  Samuel, 263.
BARRELL
  Nathaniel, 263.
BARRETT
  Charles, 504.
BARRON
  Capt. William, 338.
BARTLET/BARTLETT
  446; Abraham, 61; Brig.
  Gen., 573; Capt.
  Charles, 595; Col.
  Thomas, 122, 135; Gen.
  Thomas, 595; Joseph,
  419; Joshua, 509; Josiah,

BRUCE
439; Alexander, 321,
348.
BRYANT/BRYENT
John, 419; Thomas, 76;
Walter, 247, 256, 319,
460; Walter Jr., 196, 247,
256, 320.
BUCAN
415.
BUCKINGHAM
Rev. Joseph, 397.
BUCKMAN/BUCKNAM
Edwards, 203, 278, 421,
428.
BUCKMINSTER
Rev. Joseph, 482; Rev.
Mr., 429, 548.
BURKE
327.
BURLEY
460.
BURNAP
Jacob, 439.
BURNHAM
Abraham, 121, 421;
Capt. Abraham, 122.
BURNSID
Thomas, 278.
BURROUGHS
Eden, 439.
BURROWS
Edward, 183.
BURT
Joseph, 421, 428.
BUSS
Samuel, 421.

BUTLER
Alford, 220; Benjamin,
419, 504; Elizabeth, 496;
Henry, 419, 428; James,
504; Jacob, 122; Tobias,
406; Zephaniah, 504.

C
CABOT
Andrew, 240; John, 240.
CAIES
James, 89.
CALDER
George, 406, 504;
Robert, 89.
CALDWELL
Capt. Alexander, 164.
CALEF/CALFE
Col. John, 392; James,
389, 406; John, 122, 332,
419, 425, 509, 592, 595.
CALL
John, 504.
CALLAND
Mr., 406.
CAMPBELL
Daniel, 419.
CAPRON
Oliver, 425.
CARD
Samuel, 340.
CARDWELL
James, 419.
CARLETON
Capt. Jonathan, 263.
CARPENTER
Ab., 439.

CARR
    Dr. Moses, 595; James,
    419; Moses, 419.
CARRUTH
    James, 183, 504.
CASS
    Capt., 139; Maj.
    Jonathan, 392; John,
    238; Jonathan, 275, 308,
    428; Maj. Jonathan, 435.
CASSETT
    Rev. Mr., 89.
CATE
    John, 419; Samuel, 283.
CAVERLY
    Capt. Phillip, 402.
CHADBOURN/
    CHADBOURNE
    482; Miss Martha, 207;
    Thomas, 76, 207, 286,
    419.
CHADWICK
    Dr. E., 595.
CHAMBERLAIN
    27, 175, 267, 312, 385,
    418, 433, 486; Moses,
    595; Samuel, 419
CHAMPNEY
Joseph, 532; R., 359;
    Richard, 240, 286, 419,
    482.
CHANDLER
    Benjamin, 87, 183, 537;
    Hannah, 87; Zaccheus,
    419.
CHAPMAN
    Samuel, 521.

CHARD
    Samuel, 183.
CHASE/CHACE
    162, 350, 381, 446;
    Daniel, 421; Dudley,
    338; Jacob, 419; John,
    595; Jonathan, 183, 425;
    Moses, 122, 278, 419,
    450; Samuel, 38, 421,
    425; Stephen, 419;
    Thomas, 595.
CHASLY/CHASLEY
    Jonathan, 338, 595.
CHAUNCY
    Capt., 592; Rev.
    Charles, 447.
CHERRY
    Samuel, 435.
CHERUGION
    Mons. Capelle, 406.
CHESTWELL
    Wentworth, 419.
CHILD
    Jonathan, 421.
CHOATE
    27.
CHURCH
Capt. Jonathan, 263;
    Seldon, 439.
CILLEY
    Brig. Gen., 139; Gen.,
    239, 504; John, 484;
    Joseph, 419, 425; Maj.
    Gen., 392, 417, 444, 527,
    563, 572.

COODMAN
Monsieur, 183.
COOK
Elijah, 24; Noah, 213, 437.
COPELAND/COPLAND
421; Capt. Jacob, 338; Jacob, 122.
COPP/COPPS
David, 419, 504; Joshua, 421.
CORTISS
Joshua, 183, 504.
COSTELLOE
John, 104.
COTTON
Ens. Thomas, 392, 444; Mrs. Abigail, 28; Thomas, 28.
COULIARD
373.
COWES
Capt. Peter, 76; Peter, 137, 231, 286, 288, 305.
CRAGIN
Francis, 338; John, 595.
CRAIG/CRAIGE
Alexander, 421, 425; Maj. Alexander, 372.
CRAM
LCol. Jonathan, 392, 425; John, 338, 419; Samuel, 331.
CRANE
Dr. John, 183.
CRANTON
Jeremiah, 183.

CRAWFORD
Mr., 595.
CREEMORE
Dr. Edward, 504.
CRISSY
John, 199; John Jr., 199.
CROCKER
Andrew S., 102.
CROW
Robert, 181.
CULLUM
Capt. David, 42; David, 541; Margaret, 541.
CUMMINGS
Benjamin, 278; Simeon, 419.
CUNNINGHAM
Capt. Samuel, 338.
CURRIER
409, 412, 539.
CUTTER
Ammi R., 76; Dr. A. R., 286, 482.
CUTTS
267, 366, 440, 477, 523; Samuel, 76, 89, 286, 482.

D
D'ABOUVILLE
Chevalier, 294.
DAIGEE
543
DAKIN
Amos, 595.
DAME
G., 482; George, 76, 286; Jabez, 419; Theophilus, 419, 425.

DAMRELL
459.
DANA
Samuel, 437.
DANFORD
Eliphalet, 105.
DANIEL/DANIELS
Samuel, 338, 419, 595.
DANS
Samuel, 419.
DARLING
Benjamin, 122.
DAVENPORT
John, 482.
DAVERSON
Mrs. Sarah, 41;
Thomas, 41.
DAVISON
William, 437.
DAVIS
Asa, 419; Capt., 474;
Eleazer, 419; Mary, 183.
DEADY
James, 504.
DEAN/DEANE
John, 450; Nath'l, 134.
DEARBORN
216, 224, 368, 558;
Benja., 74; Benjamin,
75, 195, 206, 438, 482,
504, 589; Josiah, 187,
425; Levi, 419; Samuel,
355; Simeon, 338, 419;
Stephen, 428.
DEARING
William, 478.
DEMERIT
Joseph, 419.

DENNET/DENNETT
Capt. John, 309, 360;
Col., 493; Col. John,
492; Ephraim, 76, 482;
John, 286, 482; Mrs.
Phebe, 429; Phebe, 360.
DIMSEY
Edward, 479.
DIVER
Capt., 25.
DIX
89, 183; Maj. Nathaniel,
595.
DOE
Joseph, 89.
DOIG
G., 51; George, 225, 268,
298, 316, 409, 472, 562.
DOLE
Stephen, 338, 595.
DONALDSON
Capt. John, 158; Mrs.
Mary, 391.
DOOLITTLE
421.
DOUGLAS
Capt. Samuel, 122;
Samuel, 419.
DOW/DOWE
Abraham, 428; Capt.
Amos, 338; Capt. Ela,
392, 444; Col. Moses,
122, 332, 419, 425; Evan,
595; Gen., 239; Lt.
Thomas, 595; John, 595;
John Jr., 419; Jonathan,
122; Joseph, 419; Moses,
338, 419, 421, 437.

EVANS
John, 76, 286, 343, 482;
Uriah, 595.

F
FABYAN
John, 419.
FAIRCHILD
132.
FAIRFIELD
John, 421.
FARRER
Stephen, 439; Timothy,
419.
FENNEX
John, 569.
FERNALD
62, 198, 323, 373, 381,
568; Capt. William, 554;
John, 343.
FESSENDEN
Thomas, 439.
FIFIELD
446; Stephen, 595.
FISHER
John, 263, 278.
FISK
Abel, 439.
FITZGERALD
Mrs. Sarah, 174.
FLAGG
572; Ebenezer, 437;
Josiah, 419.
FLETCHER
107, 165; John, 89, 183;
Timothy, 428.
FLOYD
426, 445.

FOGG
Jeremiah, 419, 437, 595;
Maj., 139.
FOLLETT
Capt. Robert, 39; Mary,
39.
FOLSOM
446; Col. Samuel, 490;
David, 12, 81, 319; John,
21; N., 536; Nath., 227;
Nathaniel, 76, 137, 286,
419, 482, 517, 534;
Nath'l, 288, 305;
Nicholas, 439; Samuel,
419.
FORD
James, 425.
FORSTER
D., 183.
FORSYTH
William, 419.
FOSS
Capt. Joshua, 122;
Joshua, 419; Joshua Jr.,
402.
FOSTER
119; Abiel, 5, 313, 419;
Asa, 338; Jacob, 439;
Samuel, 213.
FOWLE
Daniel, 510.
FOWLER
Samuel, 419.
FRANKLIN
Jonathan, 383.
FRASER
218, 266.

GRAVE
568.
GRAY
James, 419, 595; Major
James, 203; Mrs. Mary,
452; Robert, 504;
Thomas, 551.
GREELEY
Aaron, 338, 419; Capt.
Samuel, 263; Jonathan
Jr., 419.
GREEN
Capt. Jacob, 595; Col.,
461; Dr. Ezra, 595;
Ebenezer, 383, 421;
Gen., 239; Mrs. Dorcas;
Mrs. Olive, 302; Peter,
122, 279, 313, 314, 419,
428, 437, 466, 475, 509,
599.
GREENLEAF
John, 261.
GREENOUGH
Moses, 249.
GREENWOOD
Joseph, 321.
GREGG
Joseph, 419, 425;
Samuel, 425.
GRESSEY
Michael, 421.
GRIFFIN
James, 183; Samuel,
122, 421, 595.
GRIFFITH
Nathanial S., 502, 504.
GRIGG
William, 406.

GROUT
Daniel, 421, 595; Elijah,
122, 421.
GROVER
Stephen, 406.
GUNNISON/GUNISON
161, 165, 237, 265, 352,
364, 423, 511, 547, 570.

H
HACKET/HACKETT
LCol. James, 392;
James, 428.
HADLEY
Capt. George, 338.
HAGGENS
19, 72, 146, 154, 243,
286; Capt., 138; John,
89, 183, 504.
HAINES
John Henry, 406.
HALE
239; Abigail, 406; Dr.
Jonathan, 263;
Eliphalet, 144; Enoch,
421; John, 419; Maj.
Samuel, 338; Samuel,
54, 76, 286, 419, 425,
475, 482, 595.
HALL
27, 390, 523, 539; Aaron,
439; Avery, 419;
Benjamin, 122; Capt.,
482; Capt. Samuel, 286,
482; E., 536; Obadiah,
337; Rev. Mr., 595;
Samuel, 76; Sarah, 406;
Stacy, 76.

HALLOWELL
Brigs, 99; Prentice, 99.
HAM
112, 157; Capt.
Ephraim, 286; Col.
Samuel, 579; Ephraim,
482; George Jr., 76, 286;
John, 330; LCol.
Samuel, 458; Mrs.
Abigail, 46; Robert, 482;
Sam'l, 482; Samuel, 76,
183, 406; Samuel
(Plains), 286; W., 482;
William, 76, 286.
HAMILTON
James, 89.
HAMMOND
Isaac, 421.
HANCOCK
Mr., 219.
HANYMAN
Peter, 406.
HARDEN
96.
HARDY
J., 499; Stephen, 53;
Thomas, 425.
HARPER
Capt. William, 122;
Samuel, 406; William,
419, 595.
HARRIS
Joshua, 421.
HARROLD
Robert, 504.
HART
Capt. George, 363, 380,
392; Daniel, 524;

HART (cont.)
George, 482; Thomas,
363; W., 482; William,
76, 286.
HARTY
Philip, 504.
HARVEY
Joseph, 428; Mathew,
122; Soloman, 595.
HASKELL
Job, 419.
HASLET/HASLETT
James, 163, 178, 336,
482; Patty, 504.
HAVEN
568; Dr., 554; Dr.
Nathaniel, 447; Joseph,
439; Rev. Dr., 482; Rev.
Mr., 478; Samuel, 437.
HAYWOOD
Samuel, 419.
HAZLETINE
439.
HEARSEY
James, 419.
HEASLENG
Oliver, 504.
HEATH
Daniel, 421; Joshua,
428; Stephen, 504.
HELLSTEDT
Charles, 66.
HENDERSON
Alexander, 63; Capt.
Howard, 263.
HENRY
Samuel, 406.

HICKEY
   Betty, 130, 250, 457, 559;
   Capt. James, 106, 250;
   Elizabeth, 120; James,
   120, 130.
HIDE
   Eliha, 421.
HIGHT
   Alice, 248, 378; Charles,
   378.
HILL
   Aaron, 29, 60, 328, 482;
   Capt. Elisha, 458; Capt.
   Reuben, 595; Col., 493;
   Col. James, 392, 425,
   475; Daniel, 262;
   Jeremiah, 100; John, 53;
   Lt. Jeremiah, 458;
   Samuel, 113, 215, 431,
   471, 508.
HILLEGAS
   Michael, 499.
HILTON
   Edward, 278; William,
   574.
HOAG
   Enoch, 504.
HOGDON
   Caleb, 428.
HOGG
   John, 419.
HOIT
   Ebenezer, 421; Jabez,
   419; Nathan, 419;
   Nathan Jr., 428.
HOLBROOK
   James, 574; Joseph, 589.

HOLE
   John, 89, 183.
HOLLISTER
   545.
HOLMAN
   208.
HOLMES
   421; Lemuel, 122;
   Samuel, 338.
HOLTEN
   Samuel, 5.
HOMANS
   George S., 361, 561;
   Mrs., 463, 601.
HOOD
   Daniel, 183.
HOOK
   Moses, 338, 419.
HOOPER
   511, 557; Capt., 592;
   Nath., 89; Rev. William,
   595; William, 439.
HORNE
   Mr., 190.
HORNEY
   381; Capt., 542; Gilbert,
   4, 290, 394, 504.
HOSLEY
   James, 419.
HOUGH
   Capt. David, 595.
HOWARD
   Joshua, 102.
HOWE
   George, 76, 286, 482;
   John, 156.
HOYT
   Ebenezer, 122.

LANG (cont.)
Mark, 452; Nathaniel,
123.
LANGDON
Capt. Woodbury, 94;
Col., 476; Dr. Samuel,
183; John, 54, 57, 76,
122, 279, 286, 324, 332,
338, 339, 419, 466, 475,
482, 509, 514, 522, 552,
595, 599; Judge, 519;
Madam, 354; President,
401; Rev. Dr., 595;
Samuel, 437;
Woodbury, 54, 76, 135,
286, 419, 482, 583.
LARNARD
Abel, 278; David, 278.
LAUCHLAN
Samuel, 313.
LAWRENCE
Michael, 421.
LEAR
93; Mr., 221; Mrs.
Hannah, 71; Samuel,
71; Tobias, 304.
LEAVITT/LEAVET
Benjamin, 204; Carr,
213; Col. Moses, 122,
338, 392, 419, 425; John,
419; Jonathan, 419;
Thomas, 186, 187, 210,
228, 229, 230, 263, 307,
602; Widow, 33, 37.
LEIGHTON
George, 173; Lt.
George, 172.

LESLIE
George, 439.
LEVIUS
Peter, 135.
LEWES
John, 184.
LEWIS
189, 257; Abigail, 223;
Capt. John, 244;
Thomas W., 183.
LIBBEY
446; George, 291;
Jeremiah, 8, 76, 103,
286, 343, 370, 376, 419,
482; John, 71, 150; Maj.
Jeremiah, 458; Mrs.
Mary, 150; Reuben, 122.
LIGHT
Mrs. Hannah, 118.
LINCOLN
Maj. General, 140.
LITTLE
Edward S., 437; Moses,
419, 428; Samuel, 419.
LIVERMORE
George W., 421; Judge,
466, 476, 595; Samuel,
419, 466, 509, 592, 599.
LIVIUS
George, 263; Peter, 263.
LOCK
James, 89.
LONG
43, 88, 584; Mrs. Mary,
141; Peirce, 141, 425,
599; Pierce, 339, 595.
LONGER
526.

LORD
166, 214, 237, 285;
Mark, 50; Paul, 50;
Thomas, 144.
LOUGER
568.
LOVE
Lovelace, 18.
LOVEJOY
Abiel, 200.
LOVELL
Col. Nash, 338.
LOVET/LOVETT
433, 436, 468, 469;
William, 183.
LOVEWELL
Jonathan, 419; Noah,
425.
LOW
226; Edward, 406.
LOWD
Abigail, 406; William,
406.
LUNT
Daniel, 76, 286, 482.

M
MacGREGORE
James, 275; Robert, 122,
419.
MACK
Silas, 338.
MACKLIN
Robert, 452.
MADDEN
George, 168.
MAGILL
Robert, 183.

MAIN
Josiah, 419.
MANN
Benjamin, 338, 419;
Jacob, 439.
MANNING
43, 88, 165, 198, 232,
310, 385, 420, 446, 503,
511, 543; Thomas, 10.
MANSFIELD
Isaac, 437.
MARCH
Clement, 76, 286, 482,
504; James, 89, 92;
Joseph, 419, 428;
Samuel, 122; Stephen,
419.
MARINER
Nicholas, 152.
MARSH
Capt. George, 116;
Clement, 419; LCol.
Joseph, 392; Samuel,
338, 419.
MARSHALL
35, 161.
MARST
Zebulon, 278.
MARTIN
446; Capt., 591 James,
122; Jonathan, 419;
Thomas, 63, 505;
William, 156, 202.
MASON
Benjamin, 460; Capt.
John, 462; John, 315;
John Tufton, 263, 505;
Jonathan, 213; Mary,

MASON (cont.)
505; Robert, 315.
MATHES/MATHIS
Valentine, 419, 504.
MATTHEWS
John, 277.
MAYO
Widow, 370, 524.
McCARTY
Mrs. Mary, 59.
McCLARY
Col. Michael, 392; John,
54, 122, 279, 332, 419,
466, 475; LCol., 139; Lt.
Thomas, 392, 444;
Michael, 419, 428.
McCLINTOCK
Rev. Mr., 252; Rev.
Samuel, 437.
McCLURE
430; James, 213; Rev.
David, 89, 437.
McCONNEL
Samuel, 419.
McCRILLES
John, 115.
McDAIRMIN
A., 89.
McDUFFIE
Capt. John, 263, 332,
419; Daniel, 419; John,
462.
McELCHERAN
385, 395.
McGAW
Jacob, 419.
McGEE
James, 533

McGOOCH
Alexander, 406.
McHARD
James, 498.
McINTIRE
N., 194; Neal, 270.
McINTOSH
450.
McKEEN
Capt. John, 392, 444.
McLAUGHLIN
446.
McLULLAN
John, 89.
McMILLAN
Andrew, 200, 203, 419.
McMURPHY
Arch'd, 122; Archibald,
338, 419, 462, 466, 595.
McNAUGHTON
Duncan, 183.
McNORTON
Dr., 529.
McQUESTON/
McQUISTON
446; William, 419.
MEADER
Timothy, 419.
MEANS
Maj. Robert, 338;
Robert, 122, 332, 419,
509.
MELCHER
James, 28; John, 76, 286,
467; Moses, 482.
MELLEN
Henry, 437.

PEABODY
  Nathaniel, 23, 89, 122,
  279, 313, 314, 419, 467,
  487, 599; Oliver, 437;
  Stephen, 439, 507.
PEAMONT
  132, 468.
PEARCE/PEARSE
  327, 572, 581; Capt.,
  542; Capt. Samuel, 295;
  Francis, 504.
PEARNE
  William, 114.
PEARSON
  J., 367, 382; Joseph, 122,
  332, 333, 371, 419, 540.
PEASLEE
  Amos, 504.
PECK
  Mr., 7.
PEIRCE
  77, 96, 89, 132, 146, 161,
  183, 189, 257, 260, 312,
  323, 420, 501; Benjamin,
  319; Daniel, 100, 191,
  263; Joseph, 419.
PEIRSON
  Samuel, 183.
PENHALLOW
  John, 111, 258; Mrs.
  Hannah, 242; Richard
  Wibird, 36, 111; Samuel,
  76, 242, 286, 397, 419,
  482; Thomas, 8.
PENNIMAN
  Thomas, 595.
PENNICE
  Joseph, 197.

PERKINS
  Abraham, 419;
  Ephraim, 183.
PERRY
  161, 165.
PETERS
  Capt. Absalom, 338.
PETTIGROW
  John, 491.
PETTINGALE
  Matthew, 419.
PEVERLY
  Richard, 76, 286, 482.
PHELPS
  Davenport, 383, 421,
  428.
PHILBRICK
  James, 421; Samuel,
  419.
PHILLIIPS
  John, 437; Samuel, 437.
PICKERING
  Capt. John, 184;
  Ephraim, 122, 419;
  John, 76, 122, 183, 286,
  338, 419,
  437, 475, 482, 514, 595,
  599; John Jr., 278.
PIERCE
  373, 486, 511, 584;
  Daniel, 129; Dr. Daniel,
  258; John, 70; George,
  129, 437.
PIKE
  James, 439; Joshua, 370,
  524; Nathaniel, 574.
PILE
  564.

PILLSBURY
Samuel, 213.
PINKHAM
Thomas, 213.
PIPER
Asa, 439; Thomas, 460.
PITMAN
John, 76, 286, 482.
PLACE
David, 425; Mrs.
Christian, 485; Samuel,
234, 485.
PLUMMER
John, 419; William, 122.
POLLACK
Isaac, 219.
POOR/POORE
Eliphalet, 419; George,
504.
PORTER
Huntington, 437; John,
437; Nathaniel, 439.
POTTER
Isaiah, 439.
POWERS
Stephen, 122.
PRELLEY
Mehitable, 504.
PRENTICE
John, 122, 419, 437.
PRESCOTT/PRESCOT
584; Dudley, 117;
Henry, 595; Jonathan,
367.
PRESTON
Capt., 563; Dr. John,
338; John, 419.

PRIEST
Thomas, 76, 286, 482.
PRIME
Joseph, 89.
PRINCE
Joseph, 439.
PURCELL
Gregory, 404; Mrs., 588;
Sarah, 404, 407.
PUTNAM
Billings, 380; Col.
Philip, 122, 338; Philip,
425.
PYNCHON
Betsy, 504.

Q
QUIMBY
David, 425.
QUINCY
E. H., 68; Edmund H.,
31, 369, 489.

R
RAMELE
John, 439.
RAMSEY
Thomas, 121.
RAND
Daniel, 428; Thomas,
187.
RANDALL
Abraham, 338.
RANLET
427, 473.
RANNEY
Dr. Thomas Stowe, 595.

RAWLINGS
John, 338.
RAWSON
Col. Jonathan, 392; J.,
417; Jona., 550;
Jonathan, 437.
RAYNS
Mrs. Elizabeth, 600.
REED
John, 447; Micah, 278;
Mrs. Dorothy, 578;
Philip, 578; Sylvester,
428.
REEVES
William, 278.
REID
Gen., 563; George, 419,
425.
REVEL
Capt., 2.
REYNOLDS
Daniel, 425.
RICE
170, 267, 318, 323, 327,
377, 418, 503, 570; Capt.
Thomas, 533.
RICHARDS
John, 439; Rev. John,
204.
RICHARDSON
Capt. Josiah, 160.
RICKER
19; Charles, 574; David,
504.
RIDGAWAY
Bridget, 406.
RILEY
93, 112, 151, 166, 214,

RILEY (cont.)
265, 323, 327, 388, 395,
475, 501, 543; Capt., 85.
RINDGE/RINGE
Daniel, 76, 286, 419,
422, 583; John, 422;
Oliver, 422.
RIPLEY
Sylvanus, 439; William,
421.
RITCHIE/RITCHE
Capt., 169; Matthew,
183.
ROACH
433, 486.
ROANSEVIL
Joseph, 421.
ROBBINS
Solomon, 278.
ROBERTS
198, 357, 412, 516, 571;
Capt. Edmund, 571;
Charles, 370, 524;
Joseph, 419, 574;
Richard, 428; Stephen,
406.
ROBIE
John, 419; Walter, 65.
ROBINSON
Alexander, 406;
Ephraim, 319, 338, 406;
Lt. Asa, 392, 444; James,
460; Samuel, 187, 406.
ROCKWOOD
Ebenezer, 419.
RODLIN
Jeremiah, 406.

SEAWARD (cont.)
Shackford, 286, 482.
SELLARS/SELLERS
310, 352, 373, 418, 459,
543.
SENTER
Moses, 64.
SERGANT
426; Edward, 504.
SEWELL
3, 560, 575; Daniel, 109,
358, 403; Nicholas, 183.
SHANNON
Capt. Thomas, 392;
Mrs. Ann, 95; Nath.,
244, 248; Nath'l, 480;
Nathaniel, 95, 378, 419,
595; Richard Cutts, 419,
437; Thomas, 254, 319.
SHATTUCK
Edmond, 421; Job, 515.
SHAW
Jeremiah, 439;
Jonathan, 331; Moses,
122, 338, 419; Mr., 406.
SHEAFE
Jacob, 351; Jacob Jr., 76,
197, 286, 482; James,
286, 370, 482; Thomas,
76, 128, 286, 351, 482.
SHEARMAN
Robert, 406.
SHEFFORD
Amos, 504.
SHEPARD/SHEPPARD
Capt. Oliver, 595;
Amos, 122, 332, 419,
421, 428, 509;

SHEPARD/SHEPPARD
(cont.)
Col. Amos, 122; John,
419; S., 437.
SHERBURNE/
SHURBURN/
SHERBOURNE
280, 352, 390, 436, 557;
Capt. Benjamin, 578;
Col. 561, 601; Col.
Samuel, 278, 482;
Ephraim, 520; Hen.,
524; Henry, 76, 188,
242, 263, 275, 286, 356,
482, 524; Jacob, 89, 183;
John, 76, 286, 419, 475,
482, 599; Mrs. Hannah;
Mrs. Sarah, 578;
Samuel, 76, 437;
Samuel (Plains), 286,
482; Samuel Jr., 587;
Thomas, 538.
SHORE/SHORES
27, 107, 142, 192, 323,
388, 445.
SHUTE
53, 196; John, 17, 320;
Michael, 17.
SIAS
Benjamin, 419, 595;
Joseph, 419.
SIMES/SYMES
454; Daniel, 408.
SIMONS
Joseph, 419.
SIMPSON
Col. William, 122, 595;
J., 524; Joseph, 39;

STINDON
Polly, 406.
STOCKELL/STOKELL
77, 127, 237, 440; Capt.
John, 95; Mrs.
Elizabeth, 95.
STOCKER
William, 183, 406.
STONE
Benjamin, 249; Capt.
Uriah, 382, 421; Col.
Benjamin, 392, 444, 595;
Uriah, 425.
STONEY
Zillia, 133.
STOODLEY
Mrs. Mary, 252;
William, 252.
STORIE
Matthias, 595.
STORER
97, 193, 233; C., 233;
Samuel, 32, 125, 145,
211, 494.
STORRS
Capt. Aaron, 338.
STRICKLAND
Christopher, 504.
SULLIVAN
Capt. Gen., 461;
Ebenezer, 80; Gen.
John, 122; Gen., 54, 209;
Hon. John, 595; J., 392,
393; James, 264, 429;
John, 11, 89, 122, 274,
279, 313, 314, 315, 329,
419, 425, 444, 465, 497,
509, 513, 527, 573;

SULLIVAN (cont.)
Maj. Gen., 48, 139, 190;
Mrs. Mehetabel, 263;
Paul James, 183;
President, 466, 475, 476,
519, 599.
SUMNER
Capt. Benjamin, 122.
SWAIN
Rhoda, 117.
SWAZEY
Benjamin, 173.
SWEAT
Dearborn, 371.
SYMES
Daniel, 518.
STOODLEY
J., 524.

T
TAB
Thomas, 89.
TAINTER
Jedediah, 595.
TALLANT
Hugh, 278.
TALTON
569.
TANNER
John, 89.
TARLTON
Elias, 118.
TASH
Thomas, 122, 419.
TASKER
John, 419.
TAYLOR
446; Benjamin, 460;

WARDROBE
218, 318, 327, 412, 430, 597.
WARNER
74; Daniel, 263; Jonathan, 278, 475.
WATERS
Charles, 76, 269, 286, 326, 482; Cornelius, 439; George, 596; Samuel, 100, 578.
WEARE
Jonathan, 419; Lt., 444; Mesech, 66; Meshech, 108, 183, 188, 263, 289; Redford, 289; Samuel, 419; Thomas W., 289.
WEATHERWISE
226;
WEBB
Azariah, 382, 425;
WEBSTER
Col., 393; David, 421; Eben., 335, 428; Ebenezer, 122, 332, 335, 419; Eben'r, 419; Mr., 375; Sarah, 313.
WEED
Elisha, 64; Moses, 64; Nathaniel, 64; Orlando, 64; Orlando Jr., 64.
WEEKS
Capt. John, 595; Dr. Ichabod, 595; John, 30, 419; Joshua, 419; William, 21, 122, 419.
WELCH/WELSH
35, 170, 237, 266, 318,

WELCH/WELSH (cont.)
327; Col. J., 338; Joseph, 419.
WENDELL
John, 504.
WENTWORTH Benjamin, 437; Benning, 186; Capt. George, 76, 286; Col., 52, 126, 493; Col. John, 263; Col. Michael, 465; Gov., 240; Gov. B., 186; Gov. Benning, 263; Hunking, 596; John, 122, 188, 419, 437, 460; Jona., 425; Joshua, 54, 76, 122, 279, 286, 332, 419, 466, 475, 482, 509, 594, 599; Maj. John, 263; Maj. Jona., 122; Mark H., 186, 263; Mark Hunting, 188, 245; Mrs. Margaret, 596; Richard, 521; Samuel, 186, 263.
WEST
Benjamin, 419, 421, 592, 595.
WHEATLEY
John, 421.
WHEELER
Nehemiah, 419; Soloman, 419.
WHEELOCK
Eleazer, 199; James, 199; President, 406; Rev. John, 504.
WHIPPLE
Col., 493; Col. John, 122; General, 76;